WINSLOW HOMER IN THE 1870s

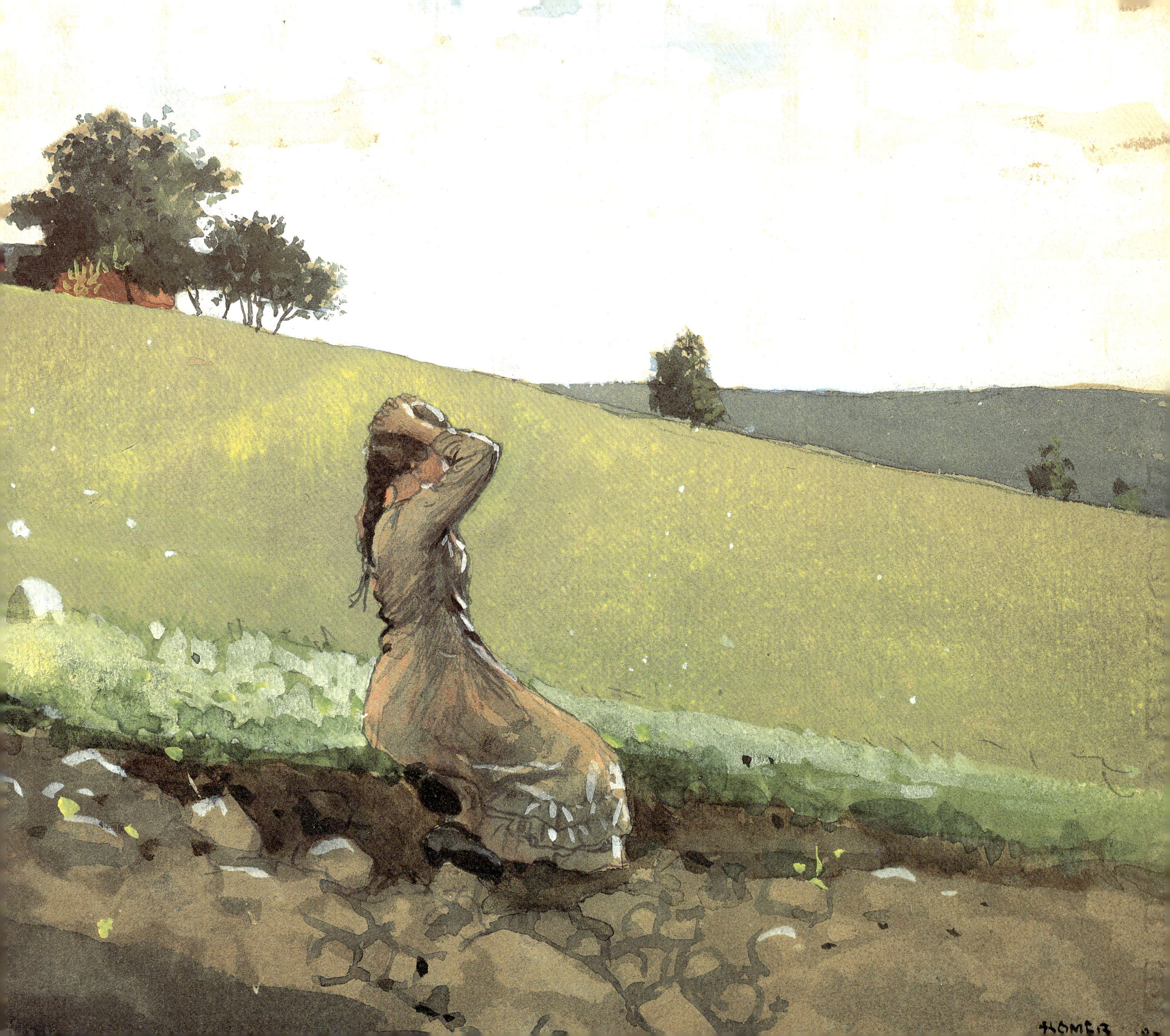
HOMER

WINSLOW HOMER
IN THE 1870S

Selections from the Valentine-Pulsifer Collection

John Wilmerding and Linda Ayres

with Frederick Ilchman, Douglas Nickel, and Robert Wolterstorff

THE ART MUSEUM, PRINCETON UNIVERSITY

Distributed by University Press of New England

Hanover and London

This book has been published on the occasion of the exhibition
"Winslow Homer in the 1870s: Selections from the Valentine-Pulsifer Collection."

The Art Museum, Princeton University
February 10–March 11, 1990

Wadsworth Atheneum, Hartford, Connecticut
March 18–April 15, 1990

Copyright © 1990 by the Trustees of Princeton University. All rights reserved.
No part of this book may be reproduced in any form or by any electronic or
mechanical means including information storage and retrieval systems without
permission in writing from The Art Museum, Princeton University, except
by a reviewer, who may quote brief passages in a review.

Paper and cloth editions published by The Art Museum, Princeton University,
Princeton, New Jersey 08544-1018

Distributed by University Press of New England, Hanover and London

Managing Editor, Jill Guthrie
Editor, Barbara J. Anderman
Designer, Bruce Campbell
Set in type and printed by Meriden-Stinehour Press

Library of Congress Catalog Card Number 89-81414
ISBN 0-943012-12-0 (paper) / ISBN 0-943012-13-9 (cloth)

Cover illustration: *Berry Pickers* (detail), cat. no. 3; frontispiece: *The Green Hill*
(detail), cat. no. 11; page 12: *The Flirt* (detail), cat. no. 5

Color photography: Geoffrey Clements, New York, N.Y., cat. nos. 1, 5;
Joseph Szaszfai, Branford, Connecticut, cat. nos. 2–4, 6–11

CONTENTS

FOREWORD

The Art Museum, Princeton University, is privileged to be one of the hosts for this wonderful exhibition of works by Winslow Homer. While only eleven in number, the works are all of great quality and of special interest, in that the integrity of a private collection is preserved.

"Winslow Homer in the 1870s: Selections from the Valentine-Pulsifer Collection" is a collaboration between Princeton and the Wadsworth Atheneum, Hartford, Connecticut, where it will be seen from March 18 through April 15. We are grateful to Patrick McCaughey, director, and the staff of the Wadsworth Atheneum for their share in the realization of this exhibition. We especially acknowledge the important contribution of Linda Ayres, associate director for exhibitions and public programs, for her essay in the catalogue, "Lawson Valentine, Houghton Farm, and Winslow Homer," which includes valuable new research, and for her substantial role in the coordination of the exhibition.

The exhibition was organized at The Art Museum by John Wilmerding, Christopher Binyon Sarofim, Class of 1986, Professor in American Art, and is further confirmation of Princeton's good fortune in the appointment of this distinguished scholar of American art. Professor Wilmerding is both teacher and museum professional, and it has been a pleasure for me and for the staff of the Museum to work with him. He has also made this a valuable learning and professional experience for the three Princeton University students who contributed to the catalogue: Douglas Nickel and Robert Wolterstorff, graduate students in the Department of Art and Archaeology, and Frederick Ilchman, Class of 1990, a major in the department. In addition to directing the research of the students, Professor Wilmerding wrote the essay for the catalogue, "Winslow Homer in the 1870s."

Jill Guthrie, managing editor, has served as principal liaison for the Museum with John Wilmerding, and oversaw the production of the catalogue and all printed materials associated with the exhibition. The catalogue was ably edited by Barbara Anderman. Bruce Campbell is to be thanked for the handsome design of the catalogue, and Meriden-Stinehour Press is responsible for the very fine printing.

The Art Museum wishes to extend warm thanks to Jay Vawter for first calling attention to the possibility of this exhibition and for his good offices in the selection of The Art Museum as a venue; and to those collectors of Homer's art of the 1870s who generously helped with information and related photographs: Diana and Arthur G. Altschul, Rita Fraad, JoAnn and Julian Ganz, and Mr. and Mrs. Paul Mellon. Finally, special thanks must be given to the private collector whose generosity in sharing with us these wonderful works of art made this exhibition possible.

Allen Rosenbaum
Director

ACKNOWLEDGMENTS

Special thanks go to Alice Pulsifer Doyle, who shared the memories of her childhood at Houghton Farm and information about Lawson Valentine, her great-grandfather. Other family members who answered inquiries were Abbott M. Swift, Pamela Miller, and Jonathan Pulsifer. Abigail Booth Gerdts kindly provided access to the invaluable resource for Homer research, The City University of New York, Lloyd Goodrich and Edith Havens Goodrich, Whitney Museum Record of Works by Winslow Homer. Research assistance came from Homer scholars Helen Cooper, Philip Beam, and Lucretia Giese, as well as from John Teahan and Diane Kruse of the Wadsworth Atheneum Library, Milan Hughston of the Amon Carter Museum Library, Hugh J. Gourley III, Colby College Museum of Art, and Dianne Gutscher, Special Collections, Bowdoin College Library. Thanks also to Patience-Anne Lenk and J. Fraser Cocks III, Special Collections, Colby College Library, for their kind assistance and permission to quote from the Valentine letters and other material in the Harold T. Pulsifer Papers. Richard Namon kindly made available his research on the Valentine family.

Others who generously assisted this project include John Coffey, North Carolina Museum of Art; Lavern Davis, Frank E. Fowler; Martha Fleischmann, Kennedy Galleries; Debra Force and Jay Cantor, Christie's; Alain Goldrach; Janice La Motta, New Britain Museum of American Art; Dara Mitchell, Sotheby's; M. P. Naud, Hirschl & Adler Galleries; Liz Reynolds, The Brooklyn Museum; Edith Schmidt, Museum of Fine Arts, Boston; and Mary Schmidt, Princeton University.

L.A.
J.W.

CHRONOLOGY 1864–1880

1864 Elected associate academician of the National Academy of Design; spends late spring with the Army of the Potomac in Virginia; executes pencil and wash *Sketch for "The Bright Side" and "Army Teamsters."*

Ulysses S. Grant assumes control of Union armies; William T. Sherman's march through Georgia; re-election of Abraham Lincoln.

1865 Exhibits *The Bright Side* at Brooklyn Art Association; exhibits that painting and two others at National Academy of Design, New York; elected full academician of the National Academy of Design, member of the Century Club.

Thirteenth Amendment, abolishing slavery, ratified; Robert E. Lee surrenders at Appomattox; Lincoln assassinated; Manet's *Olympia* exhibited at the Salon in Paris.

1866 Exhibits include forty-first Annual Exhibition at the National Academy of Design; paints *Army Teamsters*; travels from Boston to France.

1867 *Prisoners from the Front* and *The Bright Side* exhibited at Universal Exposition, Paris; returns to New York in December.

1868 Spends parts of the next two summers in the White Mountains of New Hampshire.

President Andrew Johnson impeached and acquitted; Grant elected president; Louisa May Alcott's *Little Women* published.

1869

Mark Twain's *Innocents Abroad* published.

1870 Makes first visit to Adirondack Mountains in upstate New York; exhibits works at several venues, including National Academy of Design.

1871 Perhaps first of frequent visits to house rented by Lawson Valentine's family in Walden, New York.

1872 Exhibits at Century Association and National Academy of Design.

Grant reelected president.

1873	Spends summer in Gloucester, Massachusetts; begins regular work in watercolors; paints *Berry Pickers* in July, and *Boys Wading*.	Financial panic in New York and Europe.
1874	Makes summer trips to the Adirondacks, East Hampton, and Walden; probably makes first visit to Virginia since Civil War; paints oil sketch, *The Flirt*, and watercolor, *A Sick Chicken*.	
1875	Last wood engravings for *Harper's Weekly* published; exhibits for the first time at American Water Color Society; makes first visit to Prout's Neck, Maine.	Thomas Eakins paints *The Gross Clinic* in Philadelphia.
1876	Paints *Breezing Up*; returns briefly to Virginia; perhaps first visit, September 24, to Lawson Valentine's Houghton Farm, Mountainville, New York	Centennial of the Declaration of Independence; Philadelphia Exposition; disputed presidential election; Mark Twain's *Tom Sawyer* published.
1877	Exhibits at Century Association, Water Color Association, National Academy of Design, among others; founding member of the Tile Club in New York. Paints the oil portrait *Almira Houghton Valentine and Mary Chamberlain Valentine*.	Rutherford B. Hayes elected president; last federal troops leave South.
1878	Exhibits works in New York, Paris, and London; returns to Houghton Farm for late summer and fall; paints watercolors *On the Fence*, *On the Stile*, *Warm Afternoon*, and *The Green Hill*, probably at Houghton Farm.	
1879	Numerous exhibits and sales of drawings and watercolors; makes summer visits to Houghton Farm, West Townsend, and Winchester, Massachusetts.	Henry James's *Daisy Miller* published.
1880	Summer at Gloucester.	James A. Garfield elected president.

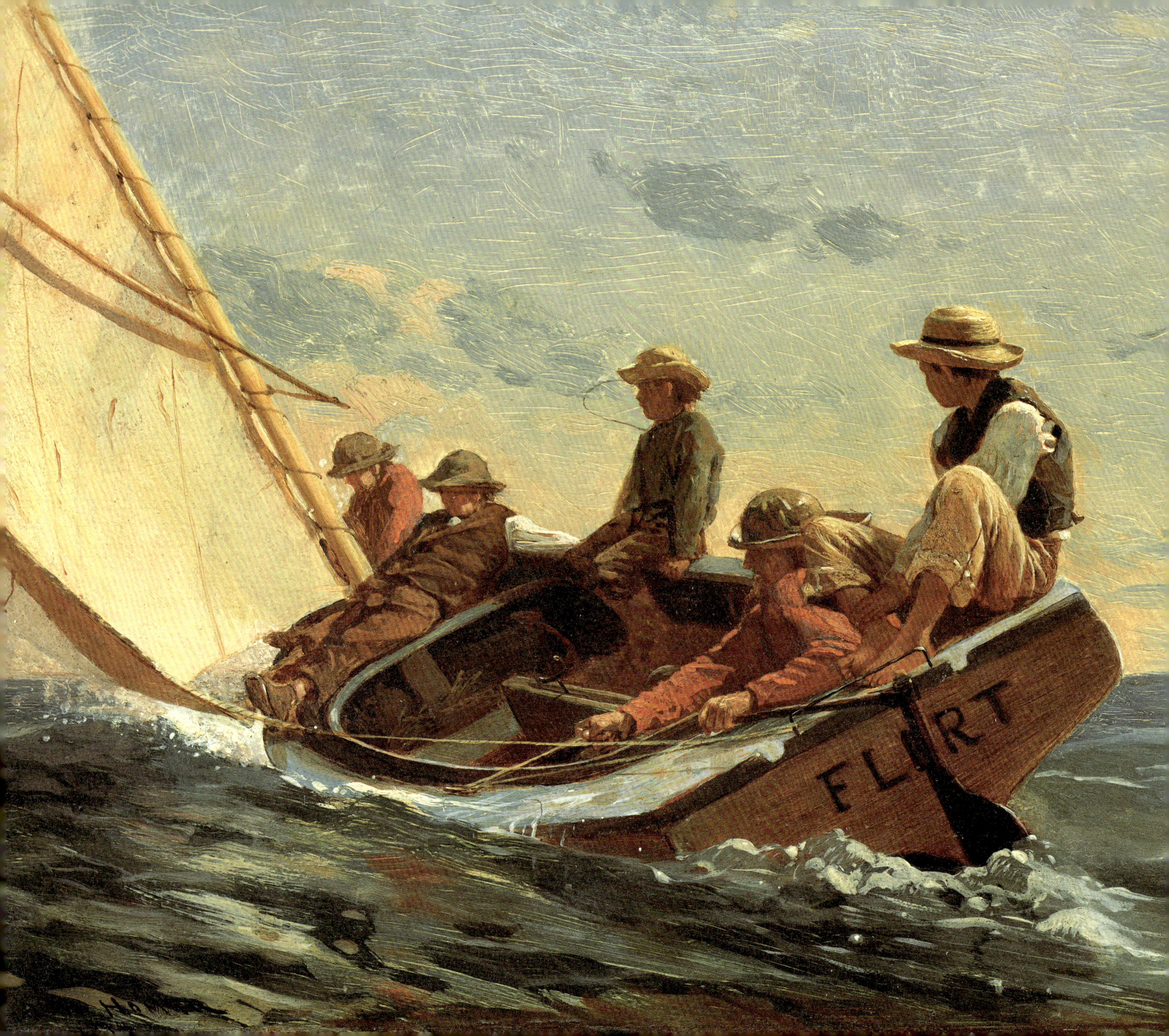

FL RT

WINSLOW HOMER IN THE 1870s

John Wilmerding

Of all of Winslow Homer's patrons, Lawson Valentine was literally at the center of the artist's life and career. Homer was a young man when he met Valentine, probably before he visited the Adirondacks in the early 1870s.[1] While the details of the association between Homer and the Valentine family are filled out elsewhere, it is important to note that Valentine was a friend and supporter of the artist throughout most of this critical decade in his career, commissioning or buying several dozen works of various subjects, dates, and media. Together they comprise all the essential images of Homer's art during this period; at least a couple are related to key works in the artist's canon, and one watercolor, *Berry Pickers* (cat. no. 3), is arguably among the half-dozen greatest pieces dating from this decade of his output.

Valentine had first rented a cottage near Walden, New York, in 1870, and probably the following summer Homer traveled to the area to fish and sketch. He evidently saw the family in New York City during the next couple of years, undertaking work for Valentine while becoming closer to the family socially, thanks in part to the warm friendship his brother Charles Homer already had with them. In 1876 Valentine bought property in Mountainville, New York, naming it Houghton Farm after his wife's family name; that summer and again two years later, Homer visited, painting a flood of pictures, many of which were acquired by his host.[2] Although much of the so-called Valentine Homer collection has been dispersed by sale or gift over the century, remarkably a core group of among the best and most interesting

works has remained in the family's hands, descending to Harold T. Pulsifer, whose name is most associated with the long-term loan of the collection to Colby College, and thence to a niece. It is this singular group of eleven works so long held together that engages our attention here, both for the circumstances surrounding its creation and preservation and for what it reveals about a major American painter in the very years when he was growing into a great artist.

Virtually all of the pictorial themes Homer would address in the 1870s are present in the Valentine group. Technically, one of the oils, *Army Teamsters* (cat. no. 2), and its preliminary drawing, date from just prior to this time. *Army Teamsters* was a second, amplified version of this subject, painted after the Civil War at Lawson Valentine's specific request. The imagery of blacks had of course engaged Homer's interest during the war years, when he was on assignment as an illustrator among army lines for *Harper's Weekly* magazine, but it was a complex and important subject to which the artist returned on several occasions during the Reconstruction period. He produced a number of compelling oils and watercolors of blacks in the south in the later 1870s, which the art historical literature has only recently begun to probe and illuminate.[3] This was only one of many subjects for Homer in this period in which he was steadily moving from illustration and caricature to a serious, even profound, genre painting.

His watercolor of *A Sick Chicken* (cat. no. 6) and the 1878 gouaches of young girls as shepherdesses at Houghton Farm belong to a much larger group of works developed in this decade, devoted to women posed alone, still and contemplative. The individual isolated and solitary acquired ever greater gravity of form and mood. Just as Homer himself was moving from his late youth into middle age, so too we watch his early preference for recording the activities of children yield to figures of early maturity, painted with a sense of self-awareness and the nuances of a psychological sensibility. His images of young women in these years may be seen in contrast to the earlier, rather stiff fashion mannequins of such 1860s pictures as the croquet playing series and *Long Branch, New Jersey* (1869), and, on the other side of the decade, to the newly statuesque and heroic fisherwomen facing the elements in his Cullercoats work of the early 1880s. Aloneness was clearly something Homer was beginning to face at this time in his art and in his life.

Another way of exploring the issues of human separateness and relationship was to essay scenes of pairs of children, and Homer's work of the seventies turns constantly to compositions of two girls, two boys, a boy and girl, whether jointly holding a bucket or basket, crossing a meadow or beach, seated on a branch or in a field, or balanced by a fence post. Two of the Valentine watercolors, *On the Stile* (cat. no. 9) and its companion showing a farm boy and girl by a fence (cat. no. 8), concentrate on the subtleties of opposites, the physical and emotional connections balanced on a fulcrum.[4] A further theme evident here—the relationship between male and female—was related to the artist's personal life in these years. Other than his art, Homer left almost no documents, statements, or letters about his private life, and historians have indulged in much speculation about his relations with women and especially with the possible love he may have courted and lost in Mountainville.[5] It is a fact that in his life he never married and in his art men and women almost never touch; even figures physically proximate seem psychologically distant. In such a context

the watercolors of a boy and girl beside a fence are particularly interesting as vignettes of surrogate courtship.

Along with these thematic elements in his painting of the 1870s, Homer also made particular technical and formal advances in his work, which resulted in greater clarity and depth of expression. In fact, he had so mastered command of his material and methods of execution by the end of the decade that he needed to make a decisive break in his routine. His trip to the north coast of England to paint, from 1881 to 1882, proved to be a major turning point in his career, a threshold in his style and vision which carried his art to the powerful trajectory we associate with his later achievements. But it is during the seventies that we find his graphic style evolving from often dense and fussy compositions, with a myriad of equally competing details, to designs of much greater clarity, in which major and minor accents are differentiated, and in which both picture space and surface read legibly. With his schoolhouse series and the Gloucester waterfront pictures of the early seventies, we note a new mastery in placing figures effectively in relation to the surrounding elements of architectural or constructed forms. Whether as a result of his trip to Paris, or later, through his friend John LaFarge, Homer at this time became increasingly conscious of Japanese aestheticism; his prints especially, but also some of his paintings, display an undertaking of such devices as cropped forms, spatial compression, and simplified patterning. The angled organization of masses in *The Flirt* (cat. no. 5) and the stark backdrop in his portrait of the Valentine sisters (cat. no. 7) illustrate something of this spirit.

Above all, the 1870s for Homer were a period of experimentation and expansion in his technical means. His most dramatic achievement was the taking up of watercolor in 1873, but of arguably equal significance was his carrying the medium to an entirely new level of fresh and independent expression in the summer of 1880. An idea of this evolution may be glimpsed by comparing the treatment of watercolor as a form of tightly controlled colored drawing in *Boys Wading* (cat. no. 4) of 1873 with the looser and more impressionistic handling of washes in the two Houghton Farm watercolors of 1878. As he took up this new medium, Homer also gave up another. Having begun his career two decades before as an illustrator, first in lithography and then in wood engraving, he was at the top of his form by the early seventies, producing the most successful and accomplished prints of his career. Before he gave up his graphic work as an illustrator entirely at mid-decade, there was a brief period from 1873 to 1874 when he was energetically creative in several media concurrently: drawing, wood engraving, watercolor, oil sketching, and painting. This is a particularly complex moment, with interconnecting imagery among the media, varying sequences in which he drew figures from one format to the next, and an underlying exploration of the special properties in each type of expression. For example, while we assume the drawings were his initial rendering of forms or compositional groupings, we cannot always be certain in what order Homer composed his versions in watercolor, engraving, and oil.

From these prolific years date such memorable works in both graphic and painted variants as *Dad's Coming, The Noon Recess, Shipbuilding, Gloucester Harbor, The Nooning*, and *Seaside Sketches—A Clambake*. What we can appreciate is that Homer by now fully understood the anecdotal capacity of the engraved illustration. To this end his prints for *Harper's* and other magazines contained more narrative detail and obvious story-telling elements appropriate for general or family readerships. By contrast, he would eliminate diverting or minor details to concentrate on fewer figures in the oils and watercolors, media which allowed him to explore effects of light or setting and even undercurrents of psychological mood.[6]

Perhaps the most unusual aspect of Homer's work in the seventies was his undertaking of portraiture; in no other decade did he produce more. On its surface the double portrait of Lawson Valentine's daughters appears a comparatively restrained and minor effort, possibly because it was a commissioned rather than self-generated work. Still, it is probably the period's most telling work of its type. In addition to the many stylistic transitions we have noted under way in Homer's art during the decade, the artist was centrally concerned with how his figures reflected individuality *and* universality. As a youth he had made occasional sketches and caricatures of his brothers at play in family scenes, and among his early lithographs from the 1850s is a multiple portrait of the Massachusetts Senate. A rather tender drawing of his brother Arthur reading a book by lamplight dates from 1853, and one of his older brother Charles from the end of the next decade. There are one or two other modest portraits dating from the later sixties.[7] During the next decade Homer broadened, varied, and intensified his uses of portraiture. In 1874 he completed a watercolor in upstate New York of his friend *The Painter Eliphalet Terry Fishing from a Boat*, essentially an outdoor genre scene, and later that summer a quickly observed sketch of a local Indian at East Hampton, Long Island, *David Pharaoh, the Last of the Montauks*. Another drawing of 1878 is also a fusion of portraiture and genre in its depiction of four friends engaged in a card game on the porch of the Valentine guest house.[8] At the end of this period Homer finished a large and fully realized watercolor portrait of his brother Charles, shown full length and seated comfortably in a relaxed three-quarter view. For the most part portraiture was an activity of relative intimacy for the Homer. Unmarried, he remained close to his family throughout his life, and not surprisingly, relatives and friends would provide the primary occasions for his portraits.

In this context the quiet and sympathetic portrait of

Almira and Mary Valentine suggests that the Valentines provided Homer with the emotional support of a second family. Yet the simple design of the central silhouetted pose also relates to another striking series of late-seventies watercolors of women posed alone against plain backgrounds. The most frequently cited are *Portait of a Lady* and *The Trysting Place* of 1875; *The New Novel* and *The Blackboard* of 1877; and the young woman seated in *Woman Peeling a Lemon*, 1876, *Woman and Elephant*, ca. 1877, and *Girl Seated*, 1879.[9] These works have variously been noted as pictures of the New York girl with whom Homer may have had a failed affair at the time. We do not know for sure, despite the elegiac and introspective air of these faces. That they are drawn from a specific individual, with features as precise and personal as in any portrait, there is no question; but they finally tease with their effect of privacy and distance, if not mystery. They are at once portraits and not portraits. The related composition of the Valentine girls only tells how complex was Homer's response to other human beings, as personalities and as mortal beings.

Standing back for a moment from the Valentine-Pulsifer group at hand, let us ask what are Homer's greatest works of this decade. Aware that this can always be a speculative game and that many of his magisterial achievements will follow in the 1880s, 1890s, and 1900s, we may still identify up to a dozen paintings that will always stand out in the literature on his art. These would surely include *The Country School*, 1871, *A Basket of Clams*, 1873, *The Cotton Pickers*, 1876, and *The New Novel*, 1877; and among the top handful, *Snap the Whip*, 1872, *Dad's Coming*, 1873, *Breezing Up (A Fair Wind)*,

1876, *The Blackboard* and *Dressing for the Carnival*, 1877. To these we may confidently add the Valentine watercolor of 1873, *Berry Pickers*, at the same time noting that *The Flirt* is an alternative version of the famous *Breezing Up*. Thus, from almost any perspective, Lawson Valentine was as astute a patron as he was supportive as a friend.

In the decade and a half following the Civil War, Winslow Homer observed with some insight and sympathy the roles of blacks and women in American society, the changes in education, the uses of rural child labor and of greater leisure time. He also began to think about age and aging, how youth seems timeless yet impossible to hold. Like the writers Mark Twain and Charles Dudley Warner and his fellow painters Eastman Johnson and J. G. Brown he placed boys, comic and serious at once, center stage. But if he discovered and interpreted a sense of humanity during this period, he also found a new landscape among the valleys of Mountainville and the pastures of Houghton Farm. This was the first time he had painted extensively away from the coast, and in the green expanses of the Adirondacks he saw the analogous rhythms of an inland sea. The rising peaks and rolling hillsides became abstracted settings for human activity and contemplation, pictorial conceptions that Homer would work out for the remainder of his career, culminating in such familiar masterpieces as *The Gulf Stream*, 1899, *Kissing the Moon*, 1904, and *Right and Left*, 1909. What Homer revealed, for himself and for us, at the center of his creative enterprise, were the constructs by which man faces himself and the world about him.

1. Gordon Hendricks, *The Life and Work of Winslow Homer* (New York, 1979), 87.
2. Hendricks, *Winslow Homer*, 122–125.
3. For example, see Peter H. Wood and Karen C. C. Dalton, *Winslow Homer's Images of Blacks: The Civil War and Reconstruction Years*, exhib. cat., the Menil Collection, Virginia Museum of Fine Arts, North Carolina Museum of Art (Austin, 1988); and Albert Boime, "Blacks in Shark-Infested Waters: Visual Encodings of Racism in Copley and Homer," *Smithsonian Studies in American Art* 3 (Winter 1989): 18–47.
4. For a fuller discussion of Homer's treatment of pairs, both as form and as content, see John Wilmerding, "Winslow Homer's *Right and Left*," *Studies in the History of Art* (National Gallery of Art) 9 (1980): 59–85.
5. See Hendricks, *Winslow Homer*, 125; Lloyd Goodrich, *Winslow Homer* (New York, 1944), 56; Helen A. Cooper, *Winslow Homer Watercolors*, exhib. cat., National Gallery of Art, Amon Carter Museum, Yale University Art Gallery (Washington, D.C., 1986), 43–44; and Henry Adams, "Winslow Homer's Mystery Woman," *Art and Antiques* (November 1984): 38–45.
6. For discussion of some of these issues of interrelated technique and subject see Nicolai Cikovsky, Jr., "Winslow Homer's *School Time*, 'A Picture Thoroughly National';" and John Wilmerding, "Winslow Homer's *Dad's Coming*," both in *Essays in Honor of Paul Mellon, Collector and Benefactor*, ed. John Wilmerding (Washington, D.C., 1986), 46–69, 388–401.
7. See Hendricks, *Winslow Homer*, 21, 23, 74.
8. Gordon Hendricks believed the men identified in *The Card Game* to be Wakeman Reynolds, George Rice, Charles McNeely, and Joe Warren. See Hendricks, *Winslow Homer*, 85, 113, 137.
9. See Cooper, *Homer Watercolors*, 40–47.

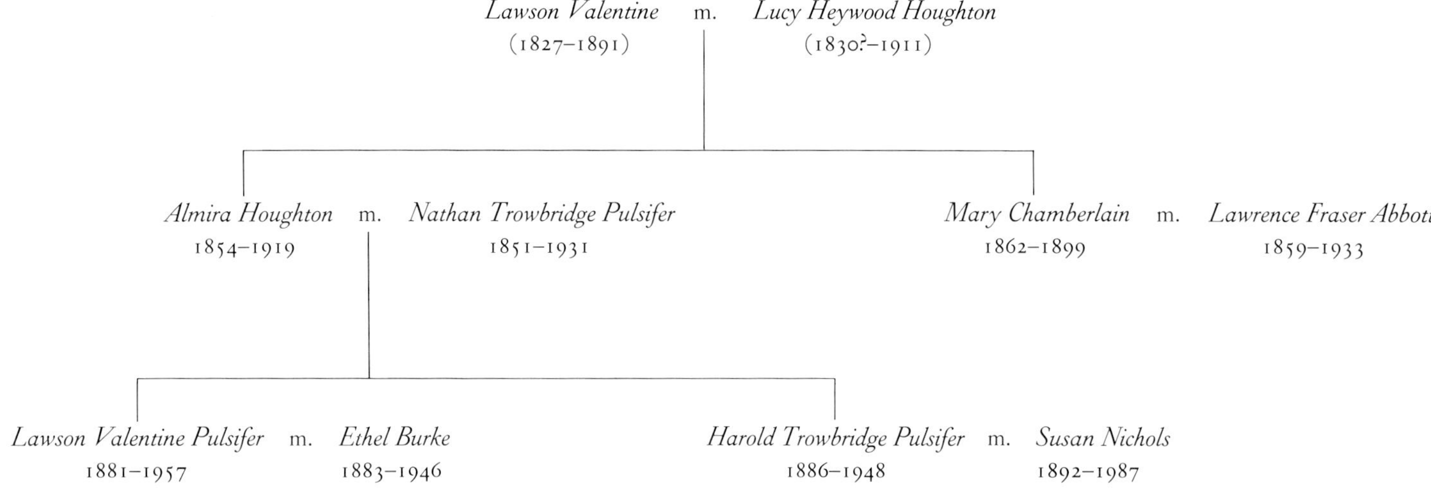

LAWSON VALENTINE, HOUGHTON FARM, AND WINSLOW HOMER

Linda Ayres

You remember last Spring you expressed your approval of two watercolor drawings of mine," Winslow Homer wrote to Lawson Valentine (fig. 1) in December 1874. "You have quite a gallery of my works and I can hardly expect you to desire more."[1] Lawson and his brother Henry have long been credited as important early patrons of the artist, providing necessary support and encouragement years before Homer became well known. This is borne out by the long list of Homers acquired by Lawson Valentine and other family members (see Appendix).[2]

The Valentine brothers owned nearly fifty Homers, Lawson acquiring almost forty. Henry tended to collect Homer's larger, more finished watercolors, such as *Fresh Air*, *Milkmaid*, *Fishergirls*, and *The Reaper*. The main focus of Lawson Valentine's Homer collection was works depicting children at Houghton Farm, created in the late 1870s. But Lawson also collected an assortment of Homer's other works, dating from the mid-1860s to the mid-1880s, including scenes of the Civil War, Gloucester, Walden, New York, and the Adirondacks. He probably acquired most of these works soon after they were created.[3] Family tradition holds that Lawson purchased the majority of his Homers, rather than received them as gifts from the artist, but little documentation exists regarding the date of purchase or how these objects were acquired.[4] Most likely, the first Homer that Lawson acquired was *Army Teamsters* (cat. no. 2) of 1866. Valentine apparently admired Homer's depiction of black

teamsters, entitled *The Bright Side*, when it was shown at the National Academy of Design in 1865, but was unsuccessful in acquiring it. However, the drawing and oil study for the work eventually came into his possession, and he probably commissioned the larger and slightly

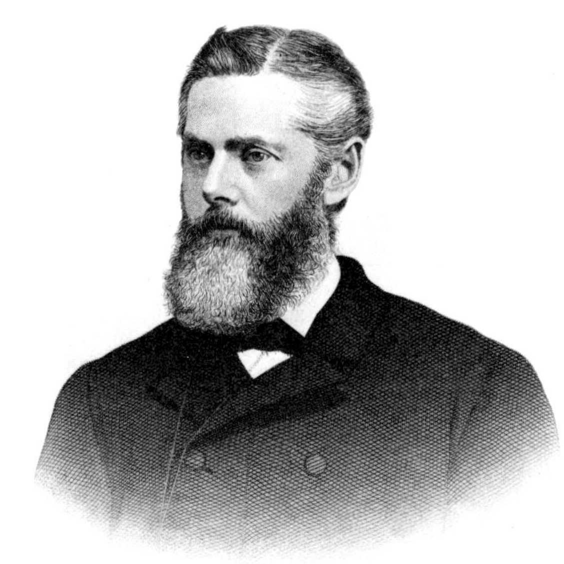

Figure 1. George E. Perine (1837–1885), *Lawson Valentine*, n.d. Engraving, 13.6 x 11.4 cm. Private collection.

different version of the painting completed in 1866.[5]
The Valentines commissioned other works in later years.
Lawson's wife, Lucy Houghton Valentine, commissioned two pictures—one a double portrait of her
daughters in 1877 (fig. 2; cat. no. 7) and another, unidentified, begun in early 1880. It is not known whether
she commissioned or received as a gift from Homer a
portrait of herself seated in her home at 64 Fifth Avenue
(fig. 3).[6] And it would not be far-fetched to speculate
that some of Homer's drawings (*Girl with a Straw in Her
Mouth, Houghton Farm: Lady with Poodle*, and the drawings—which incorporate the Valentine name—of boys
on bicycles) were gifts from Homer as well. Homer's
older brother Charles, whose friendship with the family
appears to have been a strong, intimate one, gave two
Cuban scenes to Valentine's son-in-law, Nathan Trowbridge Pulsifer, who had joined the family firm. Homers
also found their way into the collections of other execu-
tives of Valentine's company (see Appendix).[7]

The Valentines and Homers had known each other
well since childhood, when both families lived in Cambridge, Massachusetts. Homer moved to New York in
1859 to work as a free-lance artist, which he did until
1874; Lawson Valentine moved his varnish manufactur-
ing business, Valentine & Company, to New York
around 1862.[8] A few years later, Valentine persuaded
Homer's brother Charles to join the company and, by
the 1870s, the firm—known for its high-grade coach
varnishes—was highly successful.[9] Charles's increasing
involvement in the company—he was to become a large
stockholder and later vice president and chairman of the
board—and close friendship with the Valentines
cemented the ties between the two families.[10]

The association between Winslow Homer and Lawson Valentine appears to have been closest during the
1870s. Homer visited Valentine in May 1874 at Walden,
New York, where the Valentine family spent summers
during the early seventies. There Homer produced a

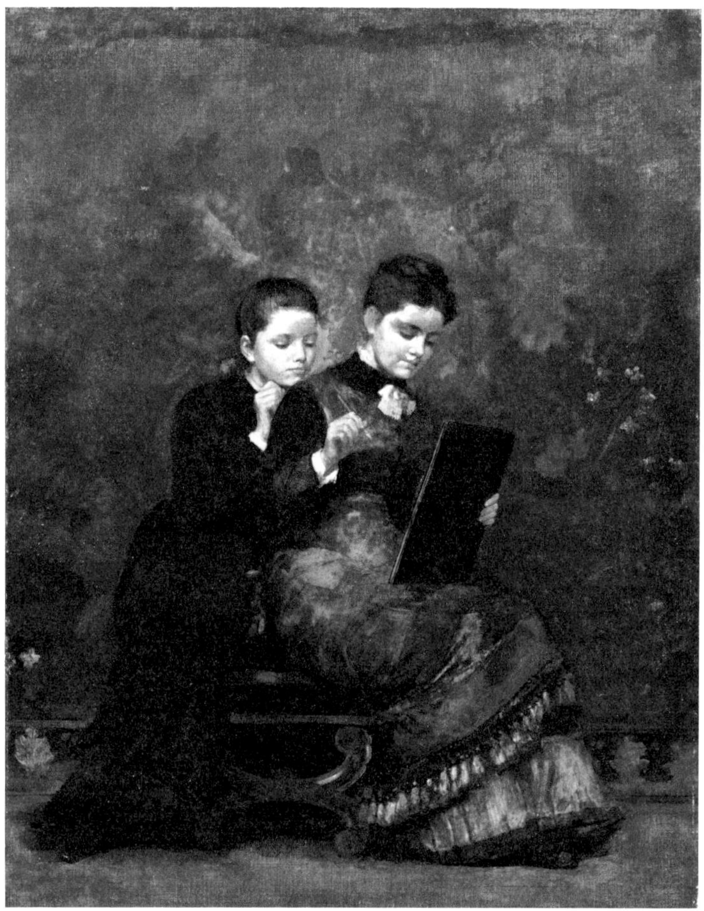

Figure 2. *Almira Houghton Valentine and Mary Chamberlain Valentine*
(see p. 54).

group of watercolors, including *A Sick Chicken* (cat. no.
6) and *A Farm Team* (or *A Hilltop Barn*), which eventually
found its way into Valentine's collection.[11] Homer lent
Valentine a group of pictures in 1874, perhaps in the
hopes of selling them to him.[12] Two years later, Lawson Valentine was actively pursuing Homer's painting entitled *A Fair Wind*, better known today as *Breezing
Up* (1876, National Gallery of Art), but the artist
cautioned against it.[13] We know that Valentine owned
The Flirt (cat. no. 5), the oil study for *A Fair Wind*, but it
remains unclear whether this was in his collection by

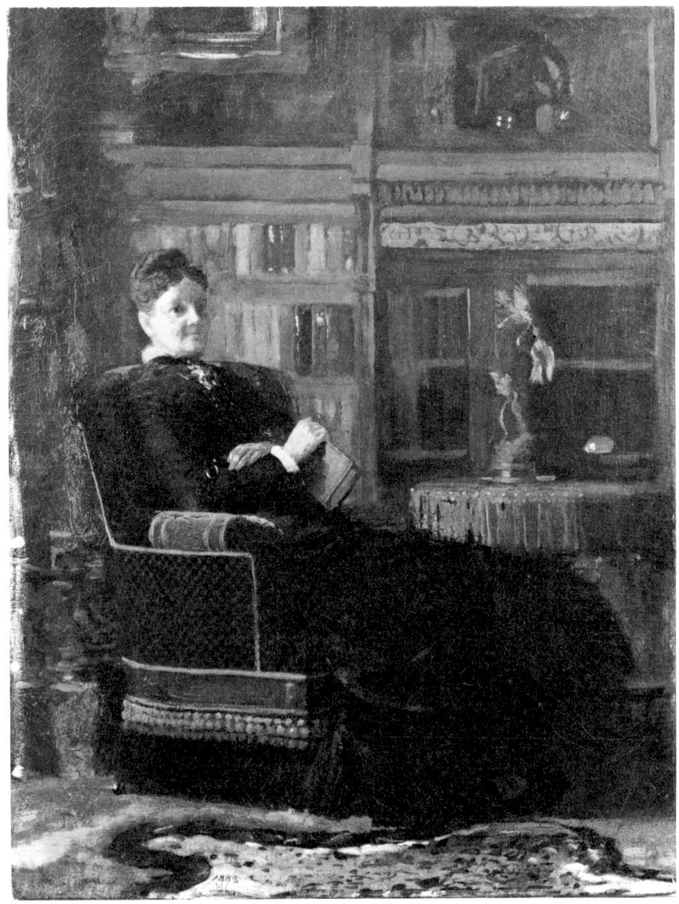

Figure 3. *Lucy Houghton Valentine*, 1883. Oil on canvas, 57.5 x 44.4 cm. Collection of Richard Namon.

1876 or if he acquired it later, having failed to obtain the finished work.

Valentine made a particularly important acquisition in 1876. Although it was one of real estate, not art, it would have an important effect on Homer and his career. In June of that year, Valentine purchased a large farm in Mountainville, New York, about seven miles west of West Point. Once the residence of the former president of the Erie Railway, it was accessible from New York in two hours by rail. (It was also accessible during the summer season by the Hudson River boats which landed at Newburgh, about one-half hour away.) Valentine named the property Houghton Farm, in honor of his wife (fig. 4).

The farm provided a "comfortable, healthful, and attractive home for the family and its proprietor," and afforded "large hospitality for friends and guests." An imposing sign greeted all: "Visitors are always welcome at Houghton Farm." The *New York Times* described Valentine as having "laid out a fortune on his estate in Orange County." Frederick Law Olmsted reportedly landscaped the grounds. Valentine added drainage, fences, and additional buildings, bought Jersey cows and Southdown sheep, and a "considerable number" of horses. He built a carriage road to the top of the hill where he erected a summer camp and a "rustic tower," from which one could see Newburgh Bay, the Catskill Mountains, and the Hudson River.[14] Marguerite Houghton Foster, a niece, remembers carriages taking guests, servants, and provisions for camp picnics. The farm, she recalled, was her uncle Lawson's "toy. He ran it like an English place—fancy sheep in one of the fields—blooded horses in another—coach dogs following the carriage."[15] Valentine, who was interested in Indian lore, changed the names of the local mountains and streams back to their original Indian ones.[16]

But Houghton Farm was not just a diversion. It was Lawson Valentine's intention, from the beginning, that the property should be a center of agricultural study. He hired botanists and chemists to undertake experiments in the areas of field crops and feeding, and he published the results. The farm organized the first dairy cooperative in the country and was responsible for the first milk bottles.[17] Many came to study Houghton Farm's new agricultural methods. A Japanese student who spent two years there in the mid-1880s was able to return to Japan as a leader in agricultural development.[18]

Homer's first documented visit to Houghton Farm seems to have been September 24, 1876, a date in-

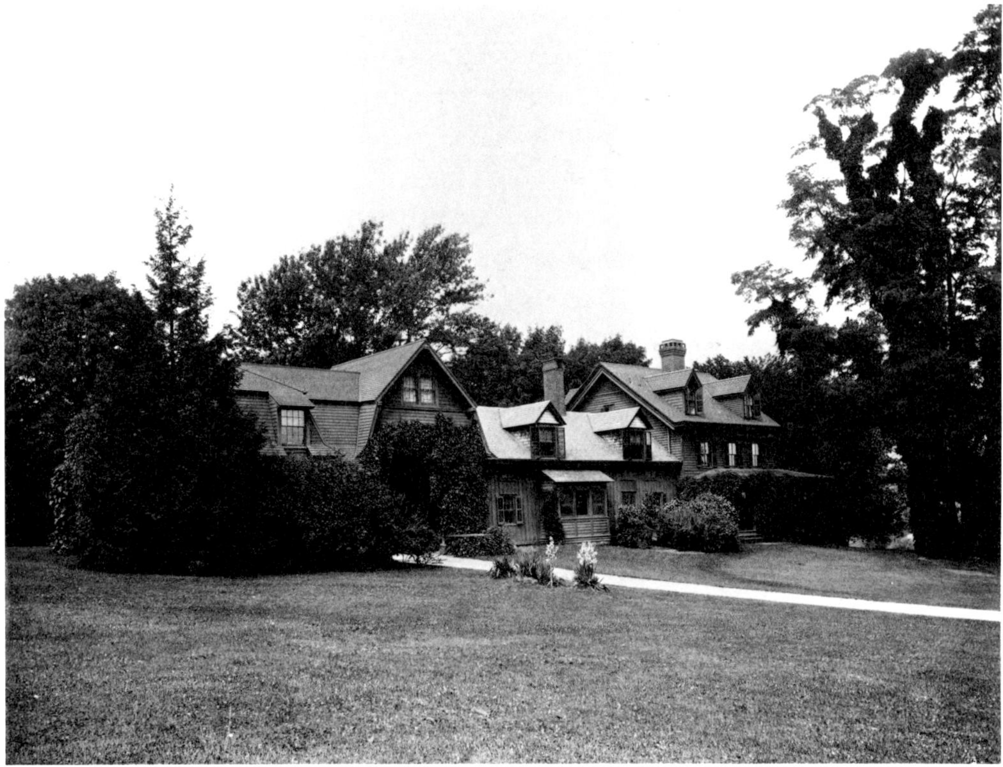
Figure 4. Main house at Houghton Farm, rear view, ca. 1895. Private collection (photograph: Peck's Studio, Newburgh, New York).

scribed, along with the farm's name, on a drawing of a lady with a poodle (Harold T. Pulsifer Papers, Special Collections, Colby College, Waterville, Maine), but it was not until 1878 that Homer spent a substantial amount of time there. A drawing entitled *The Card Game* (Museum of Fine Arts, Boston), depicting four men on what looks like the veranda of the Houghton Farm guesthouse, probably places Homer in Mountainville by July 5, 1878, the date inscribed on the work. Another drawing, *Sheep Resting* (Cooper-Hewitt Museum), inscribed October 15, 1878, and other autumnal works indicate the artist's presence there in the fall as well. This was an extraordinarily fruitful period for Homer, during which he produced about fifty watercolors in addition to a large number of drawings and oil studies.[19]

These works provide a travel guide to Lawson Valentine's property. The watercolors depict, in the background, the farm's orchards (*Apple Picking*, 1878, private collection), fields with outcroppings of stones (*The Flock of Sheep, Houghton Farm*, 1878, private collection), sloping pastures for grazing sheep (*On the Hill*, 1878, collection of Mr. and Mrs. Alastair Bradley Martin), and wooded hills (*Spring*, 1878, collection of Rita and Daniel Fraad). These watercolors brought Homer the highest critical acclaim he had received to date when they were exhibited at the 1879 American Water Color Society exhibition.[20]

At Houghton Farm, Homer lived and had his studio in "The Lodge," a large addition Valentine built onto his original Revolutionary War-era house. The artist apparently gave painting lessons to Valentine's two daughters.[21] Homer's main subjects at the farm were, according to the family, a young boy and girl named Babcock, children of squatters who lived about two-thirds up Schumemunk, a nearby mountain seventeen hundred feet high. Other models remain unidentified, but could have been farm girls or the daughters of Houghton Farm houseguests.[22]

According to Lawson Valentine Pulsifer, who worked with Charles Homer as a chemist at his grandfather's company, Winslow Homer visited again in the summer of 1879, although he is also known to have spent part of that summer in West Townsend, Massachusetts. (David Tatham has observed that it is difficult to pinpoint the precise locale for some of the 1879 works, since the terrains of West Townsend and Mountainville are similar.) Pulsifer recalls that Homer visited the Valentine and Pulsifer families many times at Houghton Farm after 1879. However, the farm's guest book remains unlocated, and there is no documentation regarding subsequent visits.[23]

Homer's close friendship with the Valentine family continued for three generations. Letters dating as late as

1904 document invitations for dinners and visits.[24] The Valentines took an active interest in his work and career. Homer invited Mrs. Valentine to his studio on at least two occasions, once to see his watercolors and another time to bring her daughters to see some painted tiles by the Tile Club.[25] They remained among his most stead-fast patrons. In 1880, Homer acknowledged receipt of a check from Lawson Valentine: "I thank you very much for your kindness to me, both in this case & many others & that means more than appears."[26] And, as noted earlier, we know of three family portraits by Homer, at least two commissioned.

Works by artists other than Homer found their way into Lawson Valentine's collection. Frederick Stuart Church (1842–1924), the painter, illustrator, and etcher, was a family friend. He drew pictures for Mary Chamberlain Valentine to copy, sent her illustrated letters, and gave her a number of pen-and-ink drawings. In 1876, Valentine & Company published a set of eighteen decorative and often comical silhouette drawings by Church, probably intended as gifts for customers or favorite distributors.[27]

A privately printed *Catalogue of Paintings Belonging to Lawson Valentine*, most likely dating from about 1877–78, lists ninety-eight works by eighty-six artists. Oil painting far outnumbers other media, although there are eighteen watercolors, an ivory miniature, and a group of drawings, including four crayon portraits of Valentine and his family by the then-popular draftsman Samuel Worcester Rowse. About a third of Valentine's collection at this time was American. In addition to seven Homers, he had a number of small-scale landscapes by second-generation Hudson River School artists: Albert Bierstadt, Sanford R. Gifford, Jasper Cropsey, John Casilear, David Johnson, to name a few. Valentine also collected American genre scenes—by William Merritt Chase and George Loring Brown—and some still lifes in watercolor.

Valentine's European collection seems typical for the time; it is not one of avant-garde taste. French paintings comprised the largest number of European paintings and included artists in the Barbizon style (Charles Daubigny, Alexandre Veron) and those whose genre paintings often appeared in the salons (Gustave Jacquet, Firmin-Girard, Jules Worms). Valentine appears to have also favored artists of the Italian (Alberto Pasini, Edouard Tofano, Gaetano Mormile) and German (Adolph Schreyer, Heinrich Zugel, Ludwig Vollmar) schools, but he collected Spanish, Dutch, Danish, Belgian, English, and Flemish artists as well (Martin Rico y Ortega, Jacob Maris, Andreas-Christian Carstensen, Cornelius van Leemputten, Arthur Meadows, and B. P. Ommeganck). Valentine's collection is evidence of a strong preference for landscape and genre scenes, especially the sort of pastoral subjects that Homer would capture so effectively at Houghton Farm.[28]

Valentine's financial success in the varnish business and what one contemporary described as a "perfectly exhaustless current of energy" and a "passion for help-ing his fellow-men" allowed him to pursue other interests in addition to Houghton Farm. He became a partner in the Houghton Mifflin Company (which in 1911 published the first biography of Winslow Homer), "putting about $250,000 into the firm in 1880." But most of his activities grew out of his part-time residency in Orange County. He helped to establish a village newspaper in nearby Cornwall, and he was president of the Rural Publishing Company (publishers of *Rural New-Yorker* and *American Garden*). In 1885 he became president of the Christian Union Company and principal owner of its newspaper, *Christian Union*, later *The Out-look*.[29]

Valentine died of heart failure at Houghton Farm on the evening of May 5, 1891. He was sixty-four. The *New York Times* commended his charitable nature, noting that "many men now prominent in art and business life owe their starts to him."[30] Eulogized by the Reverend Lyman Abbott as an inspiration who drew the "best out of men,"[31] at the funeral held at the farm three days later, Valentine was interred in Mount Auburn Cemetery in Cambridge. (Winslow Homer was also buried there in 1910.) After his death, his elder daughter Almira and her husband, Nathan Trowbridge Pulsifer, took over Houghton Farm, retiring there around 1930. The farm then passed to their sons, Harold Trowbridge Pulsifer and Lawson Valentine Pulsifer. Lawson, or "Val," Pulsifer used it, as his father and grandfather had, as a country place for weekends and summers. During the 1920s it was still a working dairy farm, producing "the best and most sanitary milk that is sold in the county"[32] and featuring exotic cattle, peacocks, and fine trotting horses, as well as the group of Homer watercolors that hung in the living and dining rooms.[33]

The main residence was destroyed by fire in the early 1930s, but the Homers survived, probably because they were in the house that Nathan T. Pulsifer had added to the Houghton Farm property upon his retirement.

The family sold Houghton Farm in the 1960s.[34]

The paintings and watercolors in Lawson Valentine's collection eventually went to his two daughters, with most of the Homers apparently going to Almira (Mary died at an early age in 1899). Almira's collection was bequeathed to her sons, Harold and Lawson. The eleven works in the current exhibition were from the collection of Harold Trowbridge Pulsifer, a poet and editor, whose Houghton Farm watercolors by Homer were his "proudest possession."[35] As of 1941, some of Pulsifer's Homers were on loan to the Walker Art Gallery at Bowdoin College, while others were at the L. D. M. Sweat Memorial Museum in Portland. (Pulsifer had retired to East Harpswell, Maine.) Often approached by dealers, Pulsifer would not sell the collection, but he lent generously to many exhibitions, as his parents had done. Pulsifer left the works in trust to his wife Susan, at whose death they went to the daughters of Lawson Valentine Pulsifer. The pictures were on loan to the Colby College Museum of Art from 1949 to 1989, when they passed into a private collection.

1. Winslow Homer to Lawson Valentine, December 15, 1874, copy in Lloyd Goodrich's catalogue raisonné manuscript, officially referred to as The City University of New York, Lloyd Goodrich and Edith Havens Goodrich, Whitney Museum of American Art Record of Works by Winslow Homer (hereafter known as CUNY/Goodrich/Whitney Record of Works by Winslow Homer). The two watercolor drawings might well refer to *Berry Pickers* and *Boys Wading* (cat. nos. 3, 4) of 1873.
2. Helen A. Cooper, *Winslow Homer Watercolors*, exhib. cat., National Gallery of Art, Amon Carter Museum, Yale University Art Gallery (Washington, D.C., 1986), 52; Lloyd Goodrich, *Winslow Homer* (New York, 1944), 63; and David Tatham, *Winslow Homer Drawings, 1875–1885: Houghton Farm to Prout's Neck*, exhib. cat., Joe and Emily Lowe Art Gallery (Syracuse, 1979), unpaginated.
3. We know that Henry Valentine owned *Fresh Air* when it was exhibited in 1879 at the American Water Color Society. *A Farm Team* and *A Sick Chicken*, for example, were still available for sale when they were exhibited in the 1875 exhibition of the American Society of Painters in Water Colors.
4. Lawson Valentine Pulsifer, "Notes on Winslow Homer's Connection with Harold Trowbridge Pulsifer and Houghton Farm," Harold T. Pulsifer Papers, Special Collections, Colby College, Waterville, Maine (hereafter known as Pulsifer Papers) and Colby College Museum of Art files, state that Lawson Valentine purchased many Homer watercolors and oils following the Civil War, before Homer became well known.
5. For a discussion of *The Bright Side* and *Army Teamsters*, see Marc Simpson et al., *Winslow Homer: Paintings of the Civil War*, exhib. cat., The Fine Arts Museums of San Francisco, Portland Museum of Art, Amon Carter Museum (San Francisco, 1988), 47, 199, 201. The CUNY/Goodrich/Whitney Record of Works by Winslow Homer states that Frederic Fairchild Sherman's notes indicated that Valentine bought *Army Teamsters* from a "Mr. Harper;" William H. Downes, *The Life and Works of Winslow Homer* (Boston and New York, 1911), 52, states that *The Bright Side* (The Fine Arts Museums of San Francisco) was once in the possession of Lawson Valentine. Downes probably confused this with Valentine's *Army Teamsters*.

6. Winslow Homer to Mrs. Lawson Valentine, April 24, 1877, asks for "$250. on account of the picture;" Winslow Homer to Mrs. Lawson Valentine, February 17, 1880, asks her to delay "the painting of your picture" until March 5. He adds a postscript: "March is my best month for work;" both letters Pulsifer Papers. Richard Namon, who owns the portrait of Lucy Valentine, acquired it through close friends of Marguerite Houghton Foster, who received it as a gift from her aunt, Lucy Houghton Valentine. Family tradition holds that Homer gave the portrait to Mrs. Valentine in return for her many kindnesses to him. Mr. Namon has done extensive research on the Valentine family and has generously shared his ideas with me.

7. The Cuban scenes are *House, Santiago, Cuba*, and *A Volante on a Mountain Road*. Lawson Valentine Pulsifer to Lloyd Goodrich, August 11, 1939, states that "Charles Homer gave two or three watercolors to Valentine & Co.," which were then hanging in the office of the president. In a subsequent letter, April 30, 1949, Pulsifer describes the watercolors, now at Houghton Farm, as gifts of Charles Homer to Pulsifer's father, Nathan Trowbridge Pulsifer; both letters CUNY/Goodrich/Whitney Record of Works by Winslow Homer.

8. Gordon Hendricks, *The Life and Work of Winslow Homer* (New York, 1979), 122. Pulsifer, "Notes," discusses Lawson Valentine's founding of the company.

9. Charles Homer had been working for Pacific Mills in Lawrence, Massachusetts, described by L. V. Pulsifer as the "largest print cloth producer in New England." Pulsifer cites Charles Homer as the first chemist to be employed in the varnish and paint industry in the United States and credits Charles Homer's knowledge of pigments, oils, and varnishes as a great help to his younger brother. Pulsifer remembers that in 1903, when he joined the company, Winslow Homer still occasionally visited the lab, always on the lookout for more information on paints and pigments; see Pulsifer, "Notes." Around 1885 Valentine left Valentine & Company and founded the Lawson Valentine Company, which later became Valspar Corporation; see Lawson Valentine obituary, *New York Times*, May 7, 1891, 2, for information on the company. In a letter to Valentine, December 15, 1874, Pulsifer Papers, Winslow Homer praised at length the Valentine varnishes he used on the frames for his pictures.

10. Hendricks, *Winslow Homer*, 120, n. 28, cites an obituary in the Harvard Archives for his information on Charles Homer's status in the Valentine Company. Valentine's grandson, Harold Trowbridge Pulsifer, recalls Mr. and Mrs. Charles Homer as close friends of his parents and grandparents; see H. T. Pulsifer, "Winslow Homer's Paintings Shown at Prout's Neck," *Portland Evening News*, July 23, 1936, typescript in Pulsifer Papers.

11. Although Hendricks, *Winslow Homer*, 110, states that the latter watercolor was a wedding gift to Valentine from Winslow Homer, it seems unlikely; the Valentines married around 1851.

12. In a letter to Lawson Valentine, December 29, 1874, Pulsifer Papers, Homer requests the return of "Boy Courting" (possibly *A Rustic Courtship*, 1874, collection of Mr. and Mrs. Paul Mellon, Upperville, Virginia) for framing, but, in a postscript, adds: "The other pictures I will lend you for a year."

13. Winslow Homer to Lawson Valentine, April 3, 1876, Pulsifer Papers. However, Homer did agree to sell the painting to Valentine at a reduced price of $710 if it did not sell while on view at the National Academy of Design.

14. Alice Pulsifer Doyle, Valentine's great-granddaughter, conversation, July 20, 1989, recalls Olmsted as the farm's landscape architect, although no documentation has been found. See *Description of Houghton Farm* (Cambridge, Mass., 1882), 1–5; and Lawson Valentine obituary, *New York Times*, May 7, 1891. Alice Pulsifer Doyle, conversation, June 14, 1989, remembers the large sign from her childhood; those words are also printed in the Houghton Farm booklet cited above.

15. Marguerite Houghton Foster wrote notes on the back of a photograph of Houghton Farm in the possession of Richard Namon. Lyman Abbott reported that Valentine opened the campground to the public, who came and carved their names on the trees. In a characteristic gesture, Valentine then posted a huge sign reading "Carve your names here;" Lyman Abbott, *Reminiscences* (Boston and New York, 1915), 34.

16. Reported by Alice Pulsifer Doyle, conversation, June 14, 1989. Valentine had books of Indian lithographs, probably by George Catlin.

17. See *Description of Houghton Farm*, 7–75, for experiments with Indian corn and other crops. Hendricks, *Winslow Homer*, 125, notes the farm's leadership in the dairy industry.

18. Lyman Abbott, *Reminiscences*, 343.

19. Stephanie Loeb Stepanek, *Winslow Homer* (Boston, 1977), 15, identified *The Card Game* as a Mountainville drawing. Hendricks, *Winslow Homer*, 133, disagreed, describing the setting as the veranda of Homer's sister-in-law's home in West Townsend, Massachusetts. See Lloyd Goodrich, *Winslow Homer in New York State*, exhib. cat., Storm King Art Center (Mountainville, N.Y., 1963), 7; and Tatham, *Homer Drawings*.

20. Cooper, *Homer Watercolors*, 62. Goodrich, *Homer in New York State*, 63. In later years Homer visited the Valentines in New York and saw *The Flock of Sheep, Houghton Farm*, among other Houghton Farm pictures. He reportedly took off his glasses, squinted his eyes, and asked Almira in astonishment, "Allie, did *I* paint that hat?" See Pulsifer, "Notes."

21. Pulsifer, "Notes." An indication of the special nature of the Valentine-Homer relationship is that the door to the main bedroom of the lodge had a brass plate inscribed "Homer." Mr. Pulsifer states: "on this room Mr. Charles Homer always had first call."

22. When the Babcock children arrived to pose in their Sunday best, Homer sent them home "across half a mile of valley and up 1200 feet of steep mountain trails" to change back into their more picturesque work clothes; see Pulsifer, "Notes." On models, see Tatham, *Homer Drawings*, unpaginated.

23. Pulsifer, "Notes." Tatham, *Homer Drawings*; Cooper, *Homer Watercolors*, 52; and Downes, *Life and Works*, 91, state that Homer spent part of the summer of 1878 there. Hendricks, *Winslow Homer*, 276 (chronology), lists visits to Houghton Farm in 1878–79. Goodrich, *Homer in New York State*, 5, 7, states that Homer spent several summers at Houghton Farm in the late 1870s and that "the Homer brothers often visited" Valentine at the farm. A letter from Winslow Homer to Lawson Valentine, June 8, 1886, Pulsifer Papers, indicates that Valentine invited the artist to Houghton Farm in later years.

24. In a letter to Mrs. Lawson Valentine, March 18 or 19, 1904, Winslow Homer recalls meeting Mrs. Valentine's husband in Jacksonville, Florida, in 1886 and makes plans to call on her in New York (Pulsifer Papers). Winslow Homer to Henry Valentine, 1883, responds to an invitation to visit him in Pittsfield, Massachusetts (copy at Hirschl & Adler Galleries). There are two letters, both Pulsifer Papers, one undated (Homer to Mrs. Lawson Valentine) and one dated April 3, 1876, to Lawson Valentine regarding dinner invitations. Pulsifer, "Notes," remembers visiting Prout's Neck with Charles Homer when Winslow Homer was nearly seventy years old.

25. Letters, one undated and one dated May 4, probably 1877, the year he founded the Tile Club; both Pulsifer Papers.

26. Winslow Homer to Lawson Valentine, June 11, 1880, Pulsifer Papers.

27. Harold Trowbridge Pulsifer obituary, *New York Times*, April 9, 1948, notes the friendship between Lawson Valentine and "Fred Church." I thank Mary C. Valentine's grandson, Abbot M. Swift, for information regarding Frederick Stuart Church and the Valentine family, and Alice Pulsifer Doyle for referring me to the set of silhouette drawings. There is a copy of the silhouettes in the Watkinson Library, Trinity College, Hartford.

28. The catalogue is in a private collection. I date it ca. 1877–78 since it lists a group portrait by Homer whose dimensions are those of the 1877 portrait of the Valentine sisters, and presumably predates the Houghton Farm series, since they are not listed. Cooper, *Homer Watercolors*, 52, has pointed out the popularity of rural subjects in the 1870s and the influence of the Barbizon painters on Homer's Houghton Farm scenes.

29. Abbott, *Reminiscences*, 340, 342; Lawson Valentine obituary, *New York Times*, May 7, 1891. For more information on Valentine's association with Houghton Mifflin, see Ellen B. Ballou, *The Building of the House: Houghton Mifflin's Formative Years* (Boston, 1970). Lucy Houghton Valentine does not seem to have been related to the Houghtons of Houghton Mifflin. For Valentine's activities in the *Christian Union*, see Abbott, *Reminiscences*, 340–50. The family continued to be active in the paper after Valentine's death. Lawrence Fraser Abbott (1859–1933), son of Lyman Abbott and husband of Mary Chamberlain, Valentine's daughter, was president of The Outlook Company from 1891 to 1923. Harold Trowbridge Pulsifer (1886–1948), son of Valentine's older daughter, Almira, succeeded his grandfather as president and as managing editor (1923–28).

30. Lawson Valentine obituary, *New York Times*, May 7, 1891.

31. See *Lawson Valentine*, privately printed eulogy by the Reverend Lyman Abbott, 4. Lucy Valentine died of pneumonia at her Manhattan home (then 155 West 58th Street) on March 1, 1911. Death notices for Lucy Valentine appeared in the *New York Times* on March 2 and 3, 1911.

32. Harold T. Pulsifer to the president, Borden Farm Products, May 2, 1929, Pulsifer Papers.

33. Alice Pulsifer Doyle, conversation, June 14, 1989.

34. Alice Pulsifer Doyle, conversation, June 14, 1989.

35. See H. T. Pulsifer obituary, *New York Times*, April 9, 1948, and H. T. Pulsifer, "Winslow Homer's Paintings Shown at Prout's Neck," *Portland Evening News*, July 23, 1936.

CATALOGUE

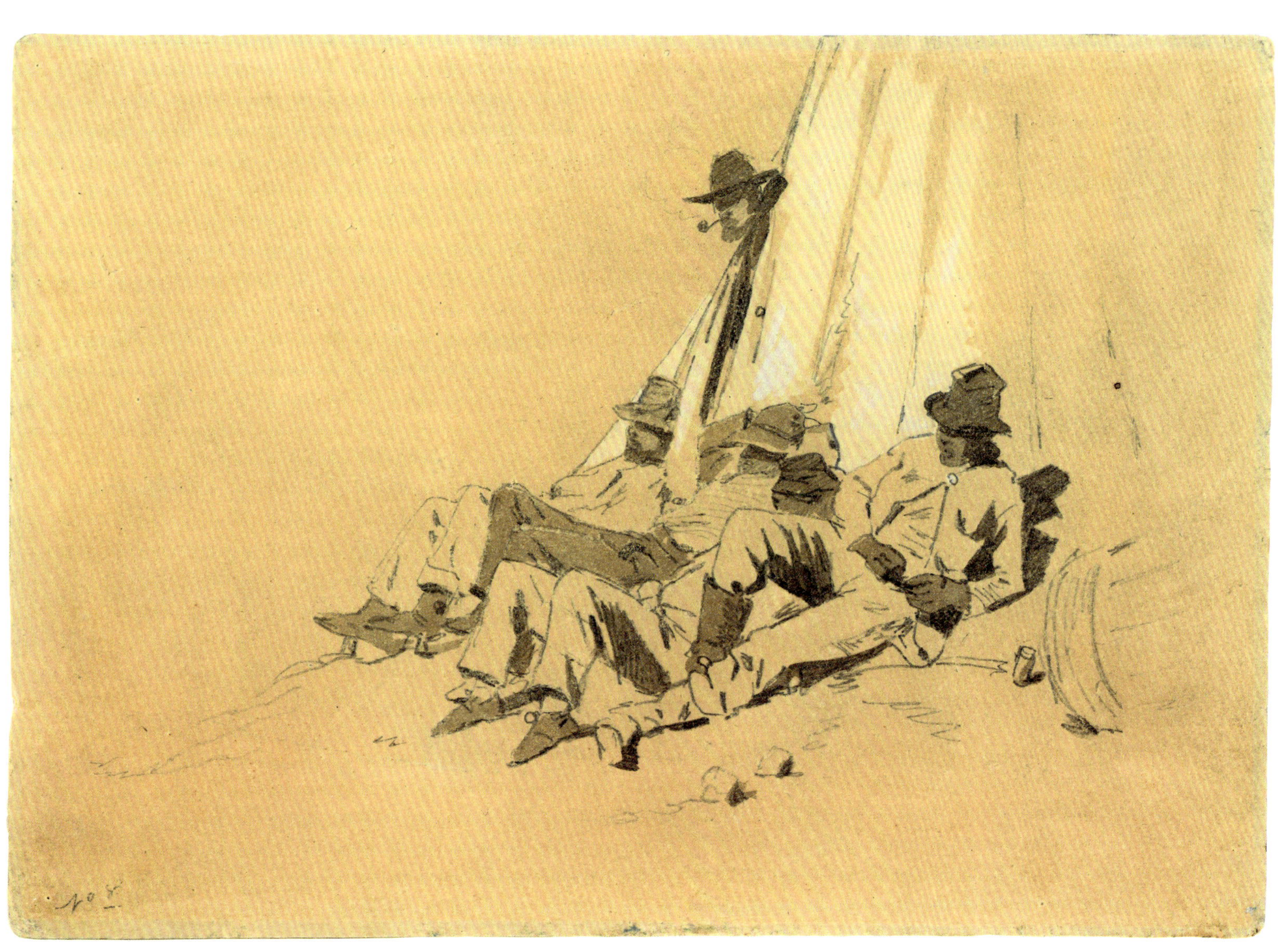

1. *Sketch for "The Bright Side" and "Army Teamsters,"* 1864

Graphite, wash, and white heightening, incised for transfer,
17.8 x 25.4 cm. (7 x 10 in.).
Inscribed lower left: *no. 8*
Private collection

2. *Army Teamsters,* 1866

Oil on canvas, 44.8 x 71.7 cm. (17⅝ x 28¼ in.).
Signed and dated lower left: *Homer 66*
Private collection

Since its creation in 1866, Homer's *Army Teamsters* has been neglected as a work of art. In light of the painting's resemblance to the earlier, much-exhibited *The Bright Side* of 1865 (fig. 1), scholars have labeled *Army Teamsters* a "slightly varied copy"[1] or a "near-replica,"[2] according it little credibility as a creative work in its own right. Such an assessment of *Army Teamsters* is unwarranted. Given the circumstances of the picture's commission and the changes introduced in this final version of the subject, it deserves more attention as a significant early work by Homer. It may be seen as the culmination of his artistic thought on the theme of life in the Civil War camp.

The Bright Side certainly earned its renown. This small oil (33.6 x 44.5 cm.) of 1865 was celebrated upon its initial exhibition, and marked for Homer "the first signal success in his career as a painter."[3] *The Bright Side* depicts a group of black teamsters of the Army of the Potomac (probably "contrabands," or escaped slaves) sunning themselves on the bright side of their tent.[4] Upon exhibition of the painting at the Brooklyn Art Association and the National Academy of Design in the spring of 1865, art critics commended the twenty-nine-year-old Homer for his technical execution and vigorous portrayal of the scene: "The painting throughout is intelligent and not labored, frank in its characteristics, and happily fitted to express the subject."[5] The widespread acclaim surely aided the promotion of the artist to the rank of full academician in May 1865.[6] Later that summer, critics affirmed the work's growing reputation, claiming *The Bright Side* was "worth all the admiration it has received," while one prescient writer foretold an illustrious future for the young artist: "If he shall paint every picture with the loyalty to nature and the faithful study that marks this little square of canvas, he will become one of the men we must have crowned when the Academy gets officers that have a right to bestow crowns."[7] Homer exhibited the painting to continued approval at the Paris Universal Exposition of 1867 and at an Academy exhibition in New York the following year.[8]

Because of its small size and provenance through private collections, *The Bright Side* fell from public attention for a century. Only quite recently has it recovered the esteem it originally enjoyed. The painting is now being examined for its allegedly humorous or racist content, and has appeared as a revealing work in recent major exhibitions of Homer's Civil War paintings and of his images of blacks.[9] *Army Teamsters*, on the other hand, long misunderstood as a "copy," has never received such attention.[10] A look at the picture's commission and Homer's working methods can show aspects of this work that make it equally important to our understanding of the artist's career.

Homer painted *Army Teamsters* for Lawson Valentine, possibly his most important early patron. Valentine missed the opportunity to purchase *The Bright Side*; Homer had sold this work to William H. Hamilton, probably at the end of March 1865, soon after the painting was exhibited in Brooklyn. As consolation, however, Homer was able to offer Valentine other works on the same subject: the pencil-and-wash sketch, an oil study on paper of 1864,[11] and the larger reworking in oil, *Army Teamsters*, finished in 1866. This final version evidently pleased Valentine enough to induce him to distribute the image in 1889 as a chromolithograph, perhaps for promotional purposes connected with his varnish company.[12]

Between May of 1865, the close of the National Academy of Design exhibition, and May of 1867, when the Universal Exposition in Paris opened, the whereabouts of the original *Bright Side* remains an enigma. Between these loans it seems likely that Hamilton, the painting's new owner, would have wished to keep *The Bright Side* in his possession, and not at the artist's Washington Square studio. Homer, however, would have had no difficulty in creating a larger version of the same subject in 1866; even without the earlier painting, he could have worked the composition of *Army Teamsters* from his numerous sketches of camp life, in particular, from the drawing and oil sketch that Valentine would later own. Thus removed from its ostensible model, *Army Teamsters* emerges as a work of greater independence.

An examination of Homer's artistic process seems to support this thesis. Homer made pencil-and-wash sketches from life of mules, wagons, and encampments throughout the years when he accompanied Union forces as artist-correspondent, but especially in 1862. He eventually used a number of these studies in the backgrounds of *The Bright Side* and *Army Teamsters*, even down to the angle of the wagons.[13] These detailed sketches allowed Homer to portray two years later the larger context of the campground as convincingly as he depicted the reclining teamsters in the foreground.

The two studies of the central characters—the pencil sketch and oil study of 1864—are the only such grouping of Civil War studies that are known to survive.[14] Homer presumably began the arrangement of the central portion of the composition with the 1864 pencil sketch. He had already selected the poses of the five figures by this time; perhaps he drew from life, since he modified neither the positions nor the outfits of the teamsters in the later redactions. In this sketch he determined (or confirmed) the treatment of light and shadow over the supine bodies of the men, whose features he would maintain until the final finished oils. In this drawing the pipe does not meet the mouth of the uppermost figure; possibly the striking silhouette of face and pipe in the completed works came about as an afterthought.

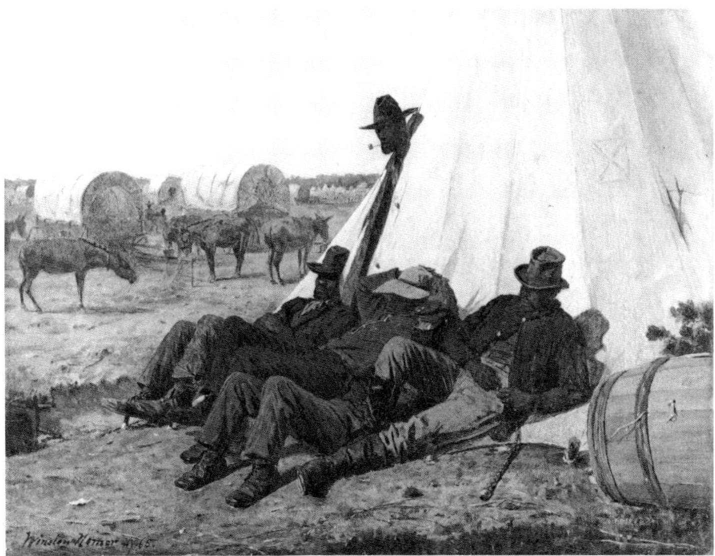

Figure 1. *The Bright Side*, 1865. Oil on canvas, 33.6 x 44.4 cm. The Fine Arts Museums of San Francisco, gift of Mr. and Mrs. John D. Rockefeller 3d.

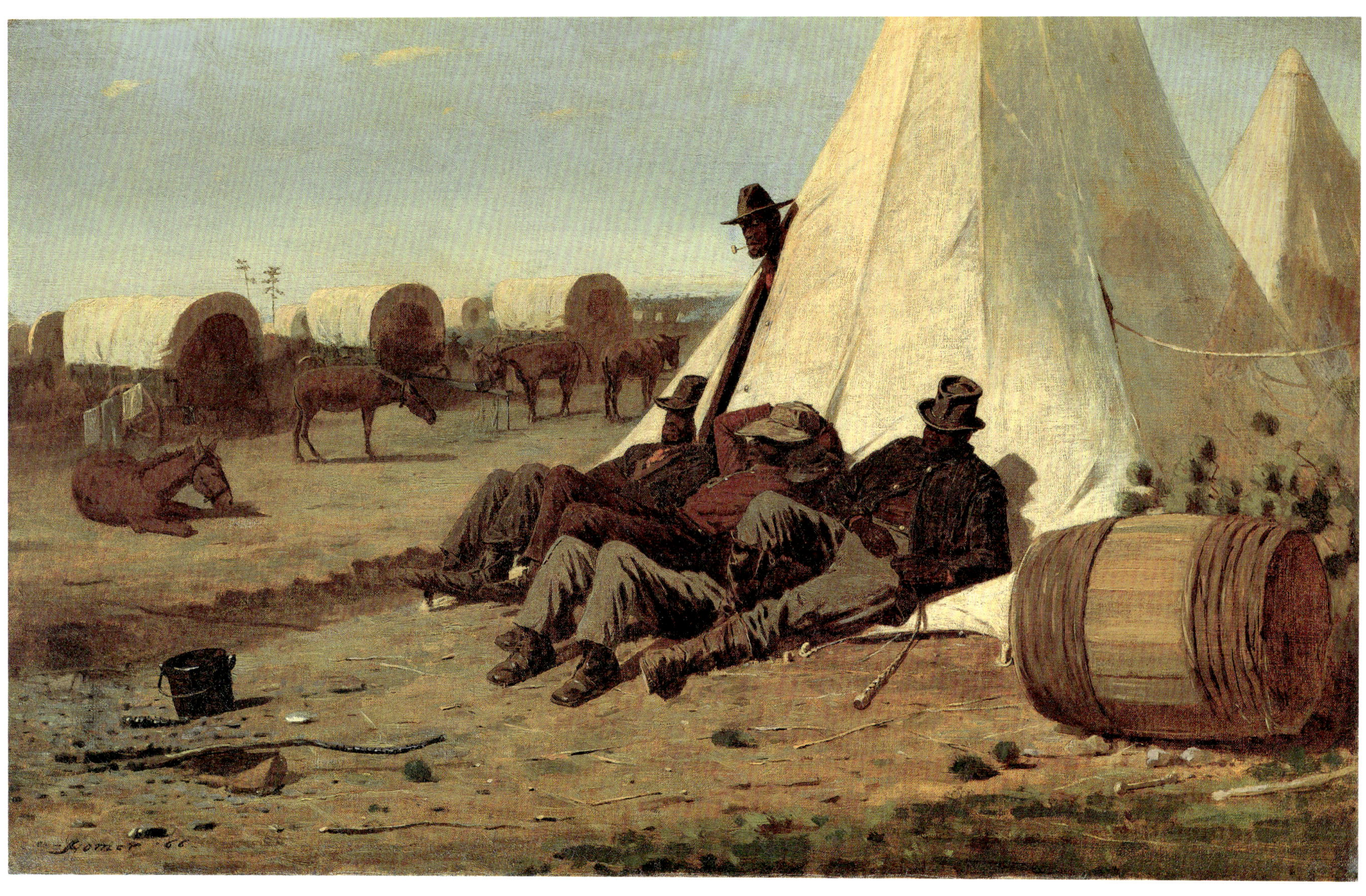

Given the difference in proportion between the teamsters of the drawing and those of the oil sketch, it is unlikely that Homer used the incised lines of the first drawing to transfer the outlines of that image to the oil study; perhaps the drawing's composition was instead transferred to an intermediate drawing, now lost. Such a technique might well be expected of an artist trained in the methods of commercial illustration. With the oil study, Homer did little more than choose his colors for the teamster figures and the tent upon which they recline. Using background elements culled from earlier drawings, he then placed this group amid the sprawling bivouac of an army at rest in *The Bright Side*. This group remains unaltered even in *Army Teamsters*. The lack of change supports the theory that Homer might have consulted the two sketches to paint *Army Teamsters*, rather than refer first-hand to *The Bright Side*. Moreover, the pattern of hoops on the large barrel that is seen in both the drawing and the oil sketch appears only in *Army Teamsters*, and not in *The Bright Side*. A straightforward copy from the earlier canvas would have repeated such a basic detail more faithfully.

Despite the evident similarities between the two finished oils, Homer made several modifications in *Army Teamsters*, signaling the later painting's independence as a work of art, in the minds of both the patron and artist. First, the scale of *Army Teamsters* announces its consequence: it is over twice the size of *The Bright Side*. The painting is one of the biggest works Homer produced before 1870, a measurable departure for an artist habitually focused on the small proportions of magazine illustrations. The picture is also more elongated; this horizontal format emphasizes, to great effect, the lounging bodies of the men. By depicting them in a larger context, and therefore moving the point of view away from the teamsters themselves, Homer presents the men more sympathetically than in *The Bright Side*. In *Army Teamsters*, the reclining muleteers are less the center of attention; indeed, the rest of the extensive Union encampment shares their lethargy.

Other, more subtle changes contribute to the status of *Army Teamsters* as a significant reworking of *The Bright Side*'s subject and form. In the later canvas Homer increased the activity around the painting's edges, enlarging the area of the campfire, for example. The presence of the solitary iron pot amid the scattered ashes strengthens the camp's prevailing aura of inactivity. The larger background also allowed the artist to add a third parallel column of covered wagons and thus reinforce the strong diagonal completed by the barrel in the right foreground. The conflict of this diagonal with the line formed by the prostrate bodies provides greater tension in an otherwise motionless composition. At the same time, the sunlight appears stronger than in *The Bright Side*, falling on the tent with greater gradations of shadow. Fewer clouds dot the sky.

Homer did not like all his improvements, however. We can see that he painted out the horse's head he had thought to introduce above the barrel; with time, the thinly painted covering has faded to reveal the ghostly outline of an equine figure. Except for this passage, *Army Teamsters* is finely painted, giving the work a much more finished appearance than that of *The Bright Side*. Many details, such as the folds of the teamsters' trousers, are rendered with greater precision. This more meticulous style would have answered the cry of the artist's critics, who repeatedly asked of Homer that he refine the finish of his works.[15] By the standards of the day, then, it would seem that Lawson Valentine did not acquire from the artist a copy; he instead took possession of Homer's culminating work on the theme of Civil War camp life.

F.I.

1. Marc Simpson et al., *Winslow Homer: Paintings of the Civil War*, exhib. cat., The Fine Arts Museums of San Francisco, Portland Museum of Art, Amon Carter Museum (San Francisco, 1988), cat. no. 13, esp. p. 201.

2. Simpson et al., *Homer: Paintings*, 47.

3. Ibid.

4. For a summary of northern and southern attitudes toward black soldiers in the Civil War, see James M. McPherson, *Battle Cry of Freedom* (New York, 1988), esp. 563–67, 768–69, 831–37.

5. "National Academy of Design. Fortieth Annual Exhibition, Concluding Article," *Evening Post*, May 31, 1865; quoted in Simpson, et al., *Homer: Paintings*, 47.

6. Simpson et al., *Homer: Paintings*, 47.

7. "National Academy of Design, Seventh Article," *Watson's Weekly Art Journal* 3 (July 1, 1865): 148–49; "National Academy of Design," *New-York Daily Tribune*, July 3, 1865; quoted in Simpson et al., *Homer: Paintings*, 206.

8. Simpson et al., *Homer: Paintings*, 205–7.

9. Simpson et al., *Homer: Paintings*, 47–64, 198–207; Peter H. Wood and Karen C. C. Dalton, *Winslow Homer's Images of Blacks: The Civil War and Reconstruction Years*, exhib. cat., the Menil Collection, Virginia Museum of Fine Arts, North Carolina Museum of Art (Austin, 1988). Both essays thoroughly explore the ramifications of such readings, placing the work within larger artistic and cultural contexts. Albert Boime, "Blacks in Shark-Infested Waters: Visual Encodings of Racism in Copley and Homer," *Smithsonian Studies in American Art* 1 (Winter 1989): 19–47, provides an excellent additional study, concentrating on Homer's late masterpiece, *The Gulf Stream*.

10. Scholars have also confused *Army Teamsters* with *The Bright Side*; for example, William H. Downes, *The Life and Works of Winslow Homer* (Boston and New York, 1911), 52, erroneously lists "Mr. Lawson Valentine" as one of the past owners of *The Bright Side*.

11. Simpson et al., *Homer: Paintings*, 200.

12. Simpson et al., *Homer: Paintings*, 201, 204, fig. 13.2. According to Simpson, Valentine inscribed the print "With the compliments of Lawson Valentine."

13. For the covered wagons and camp arrangements Homer used such pencil-and-wash drawings as *Resting Mules Tethered to Wagon*, 1862, and *Army Wagon and Mule*, 1862 (both Cooper-Hewitt Museum); for the standing mule to the left in both oil paintings he employed the drawing *Two Studies of Mules Resting* (private collection); and for the recumbent mule at the far left of *Army Teamsters* he made use of the drawing *Resting Mule*, 1862 (Cooper-Hewitt Museum); see Simpson et al., *Homer: Paintings*, cat. nos. 13c, 13d, 13g, and p. 204, fig. 13.1.

14. Simpson et al., *Homer: Paintings*, 199.

15. For such examples, see the "collected references prior to 1876" listed for each of Homer's Civil War paintings in Simpson et al., *Homer: Paintings*; for *The Bright Side*, see esp. 206.

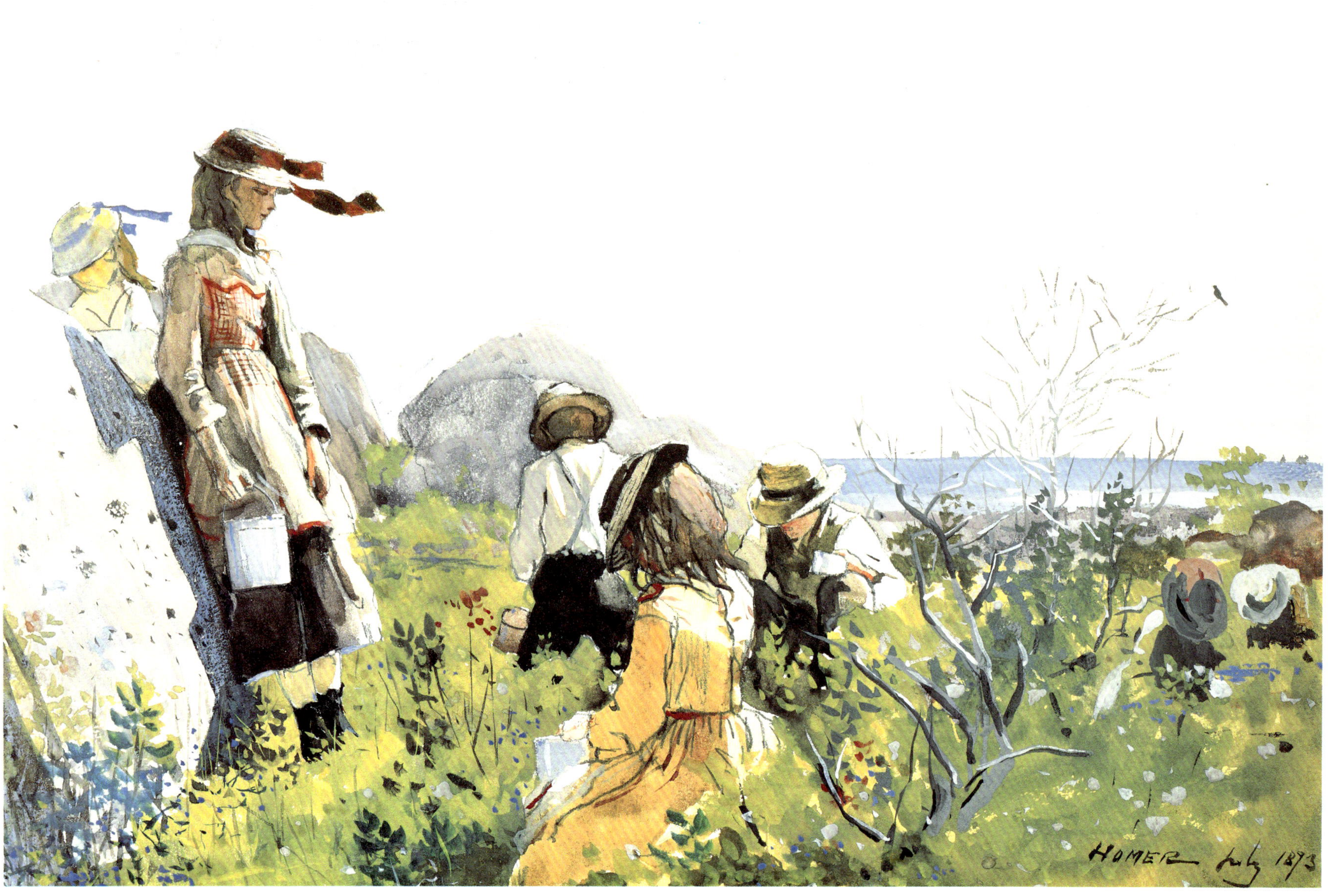

3. *Berry Pickers*, 1873

Watercolor, graphite, and gouache, 24.8 x 35.2 cm. (9¾ x 13⅞ in.)
Signed and dated lower right: *HOMER July 1873*
Private collection

During the Civil War, while he worked in the field making sketches for magazine illustrations, Homer established his artistic credo: "I prefer every time," he said, "a picture composed and painted outdoors."[1] In the years preceding his departure for Paris, Homer had wrestled with the problem of rendering studio productions such as *The Bright Side* and *Prisoners from the Front* as convincing outdoor scenes, but his growing interest in a realist approach to painting led him more and more to a belief in only those works made directly from nature. In December 1866, he sailed for France, where he enjoyed a year's residence in Paris—the world's center for progressive ideas in the arts—and in the heart of the region frequented by the most advanced French landscape painters of the day, the countryside south of Paris and around the town of Barbizon.[2] His sojourn in France gave him a more cosmopolitan outlook upon his chosen profession, and marked the beginning of his acceptance as an internationally recognized artist.

The Barbizon painters shared Homer's enthusiasm for painting *en plein aire*, and their pictures would have confirmed the young American in his determination to eschew studio manipulations in favor of outdoor work.[3] In fact, some have seen Homer's residency in France as a turning point in the artist's career.[4] This assessment is corroborated by Homer's friend, the painter John La Farge, who himself was profoundly influenced by the Barbizon artists. Before traveling to Europe for the first time, both La Farge and Homer saw lithographed reproductions of this French landscape work; "Mr. Winslow Homer . . . was a student of these things and has, like myself, been largely made by them," La Farge reported.[5]

The efforts of one French naturalist, Eugène Boudin, seem to have exerted a particularly strong influence, one that would remain with Homer for years. In the 1860s, Boudin specialized in paintings that depicted fashionable bourgeois beachgoers congregating at such resorts as Trouville, in Normandy (fig. 1). A heightened color, lack of finish, and sense of spontaneity, all characteristic of Boudin's outdoor scenes, were qualities that American critics noticed in Homer's work after 1868. Also, while it accorded with his own aesthetic philosophy, this new style of painting was gaining increasing commercial viability—a development not likely to be

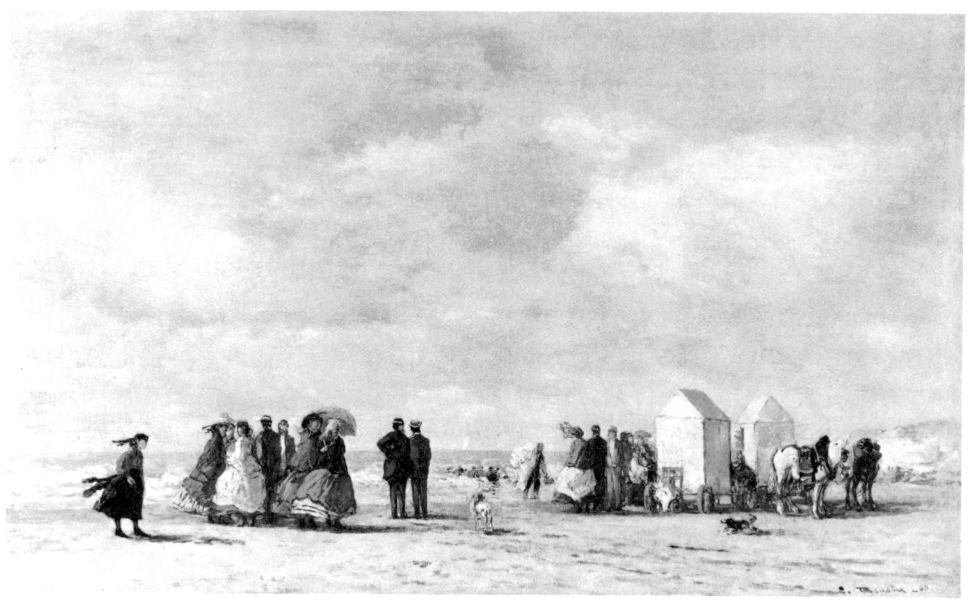

Figure 1. Eugène Boudin, *Beach at Trouville*, 1865. Oil on canvas, 38 x 62.8 cm. The Art Museum, Princeton University, gift of the estate of Laurence Hutton, Class of 1913.

lost on the pragmatic Homer. In works executed during the period just after his return from France, Homer introduced subjects and treatments similar to those of Boudin. The high-key palette and windswept figures of his *Long Branch, New Jersey* (fig. 2), for example, hark back to Boudin, even if his needs as an illustrator led him to simplify his forms and emphasize outlines.[6]

In the summer of 1873, at the popular American beach resort of Gloucester, Massachusetts, Homer painted his first watercolors. In adopting the watercolor medium, the artist found that he could produce finished works quickly and directly from nature, capturing the fleeting effects of light and atmosphere that so interested him. One of his earliest watercolors was destined to be one of his most admired: *Berry Pickers*, dated July 1873, which depicts the well-dressed children of summer tourists engaged in a typical local pastime. Along with its companion-piece, *The Clambake* (fig. 3),[7] *Berry Pickers* demonstrates aspects of Homer's transition from illustrator to painter in the early 1870s, while presenting a

subject that would dominate his art in this decade—that of children at rest or play.

While there is a similarity to Boudin in theme and subject, traces of Boudin's painterly influence can be felt in the blowing ribbons of the girls' hats, a conceit that serves to arrest the flow of time and suspend narrative action for an instant. But Homer, with an eye to an eventual wood-engraved version, also chose to arrange his figures in such a way that they can be read left to right as well as in space. The compositional strategy was noted by Kenyon Cox:

An admirable instance of the expressiveness of Homer's composition . . . is the little watercolor of Berry Pickers of 1873. At first sight it is a simple transcript from nature, with little style in either the drawing or the color, yet it is full of a charm difficult to account for. And then one notices that the lines of all the subordinate figures lead straight to the head of the taller girl, standing alone on the left, and that she has a blowing ribbon on her hat. The line of that ribbon takes possession of the eye, which is carried by it, and by the clouds in the sky, straight across the picture to the other end where, so small as to be otherwise unnoticeable, a singing bird sits upon the branch of a bare shrub. By that subtle bit of arrangement the air has been filled not only with sun and breeze but with music, and the expression of the summer morning is complete.[8]

As Cox suggests, Homer's composition encourages us to roam visually across the picture's surface. In addition to its formal sophistication, *Berry Pickers* exhibits another trait characteristic of Homer's group scenes during these years: except for that of the standing girl, the faces of the children are all hidden from view. As he had in *Croquet Scene* (fig. 4) and *High Tide* (1870, The Metropolitan Museum of Art), Homer here (as well as in *The Clambake*) obscures the features of all but one of his figures, isolating the viewer from the action and lending the work a sense of immediacy, as if the scene were just stumbled upon. This tactic may have enhanced the naturalistic effect Homer sought, but it also lends the

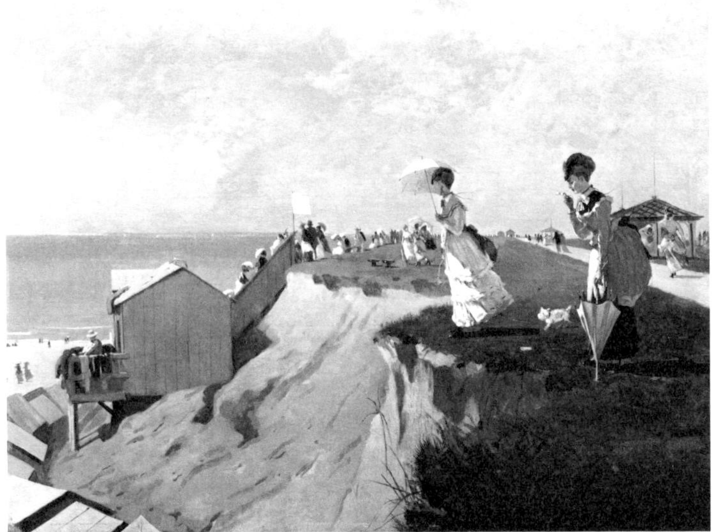

Figure 2. *Long Branch, New Jersey*, 1869. Oil on canvas, 40.6 x 55.2 cm. Museum of Fine Arts, Boston, the Hayden Collection.

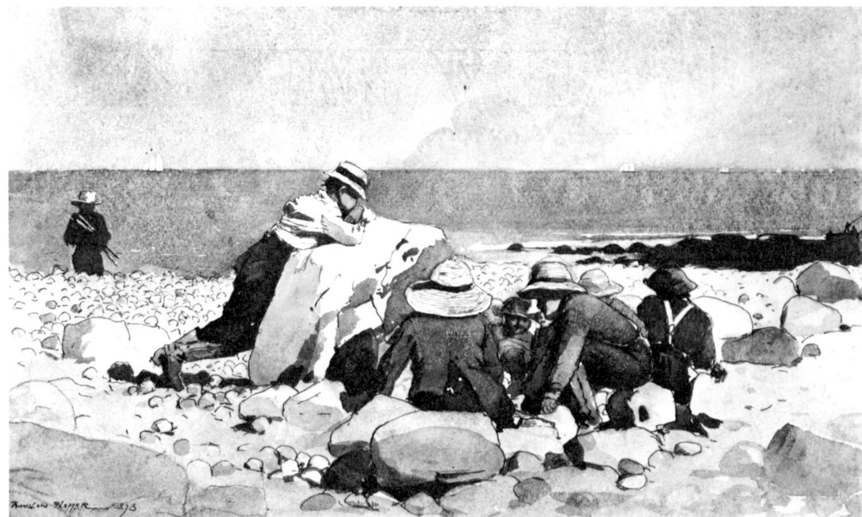

Figure 3. *The Clambake*, 1873. Watercolor, 21.3 x 35.2 cm. Cleveland Museum of Art, gift of Mrs. Homer H. Johnson.

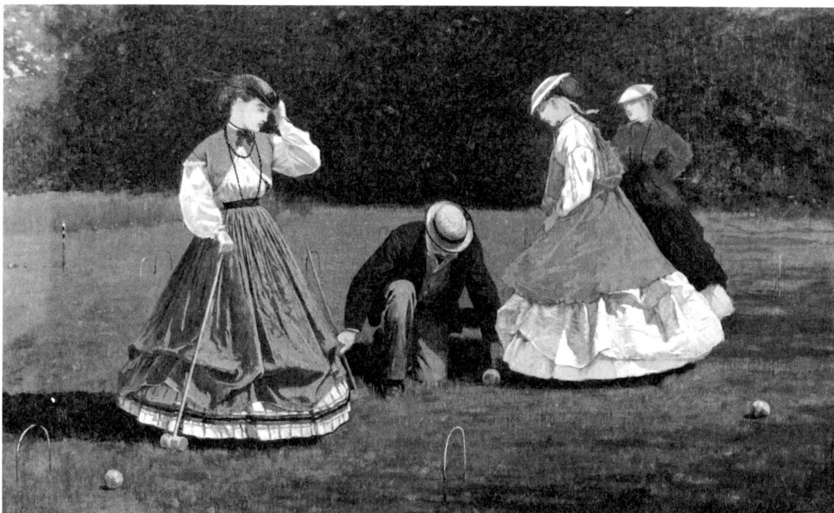

Figure 4. *Croquet Scene*, 1866. Oil on canvas, 40.3 x 66.2 cm. The Art Institute of Chicago.

image a psychological tension that works against the carefree innocence of Cox's description. For in their concentration upon their task, these children not only ignore our presence but fail to interact with one another. It might be argued that Homer's most compelling works partake of the two kinds of realism apparent in *Berry Pickers*—a technical naturalism derived from incisive observation, and a psychological veracity that describes the relations that sometimes exist between people.

D.N.

1. Quoted in George W. Sheldon, *Hours with Art and Artists* (New York, 1882), 138.
2. In France Homer stayed with a long-time friend, J. Foxcroft Cole, whom he had known from the days of his lithographic apprenticeship at the firm of Bufford's in Boston. While visiting Cole in 1867, Homer exe-cuted landscape oils that bear the unmistakable style of the Barbizon School painters, especially that of Corot. If Homer's earlier painted works aspired to the technique of Courbet, they now aligned themselves clearly (if briefly) with the naturalist school of French landscape painting; see Albert Ten Eyck Gardner, *Winslow Homer, American Artist: His World and His Work* (New York, 1961), 88–119.
3. See John Wilmerding, *Winslow Homer* (New York, 1972), 50.
4. See Gardner, *Homer, American Artist*, 89.
5. Quoted by Lloyd Goodrich, *Winslow Homer* (New York, 1944), 36.
6. On Homer's indebtedness to Boudin, see Alexandra R. Murphy, Rafael Fernandez, and Jennifer Gordon, *Winslow Homer in the Clark Collection*, exhib. cat., Sterling and Francine Clark Art Institute (Williamstown, Mass., 1986), 11.
7. Painted the summer Homer executed *Berry Pickers*, *The Clambake* has approximately the same dimensions and similar composition, spatial construction, and poses. Both works were published (in modified form) as *Harper's Weekly* wood engravings, the former in 1874, the latter in 1873.
8. Kenyon Cox, "Winslow Homer" (1914) in *What Is Painting? "Winslow Homer" and Other Essays* (New York, 1988), 67–68.

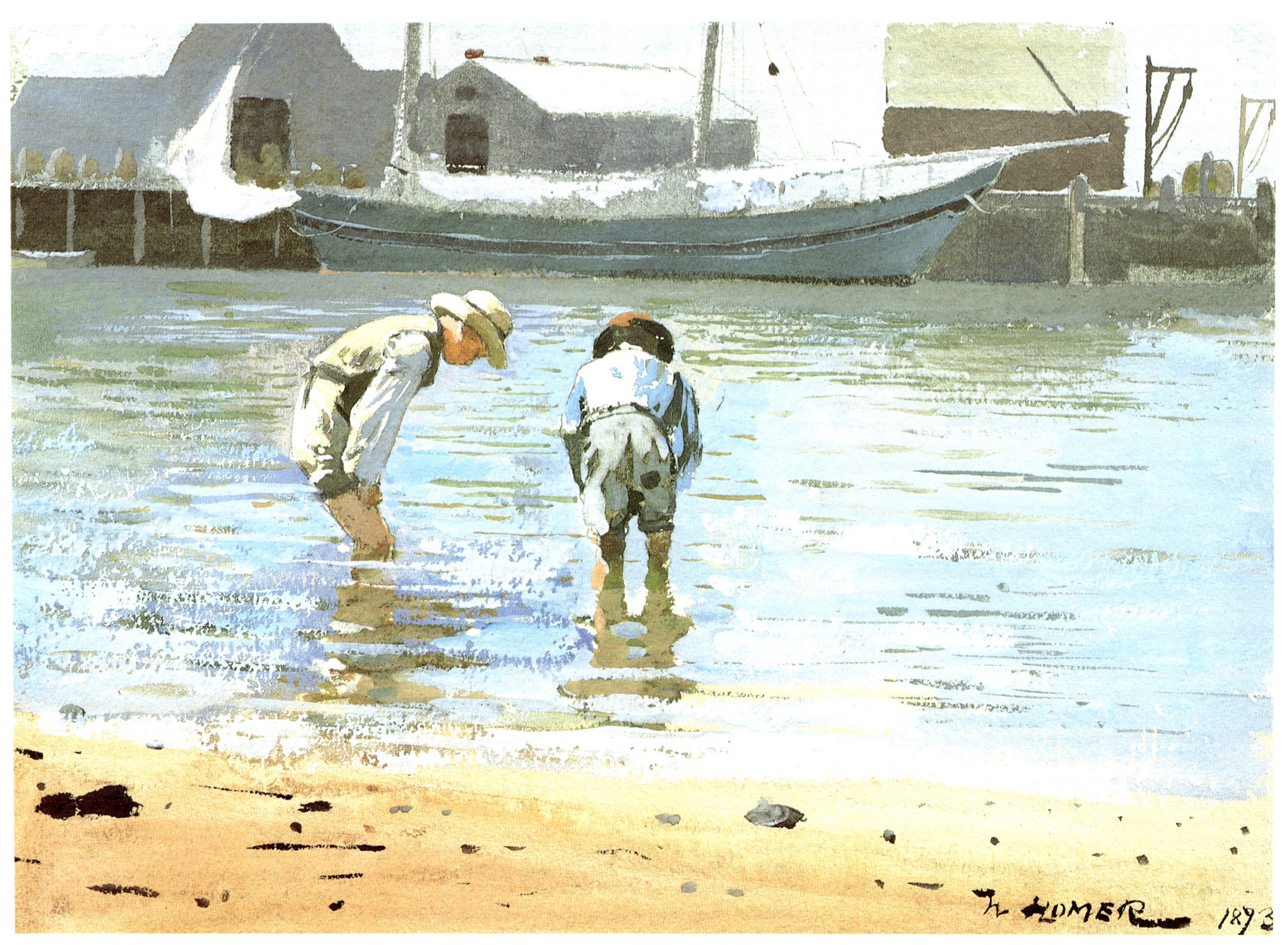

4. *Boys Wading*, 1873

Watercolor and gouache over graphite, 24.8 x 34.9 cm.
(9¾ x 13¾ in.)
Inscribed lower right: *W HOMER 1873*
Private collection

Winslow Homer spent the summer of 1873 in Gloucester, Massachusetts, an old fishing town thirty miles north of Boston. Here he created his first finished works in watercolor—airy, optimistic scenes of children at play in the brilliant summer light. As was the case during the working vacations he took throughout the rest of his life—summers in Canada or the Adirondacks; winters (after his move to Prout's Neck, Maine, in 1882) in Florida, Bermuda, Cuba, and the Bahamas—this particular location led to a group of works in watercolor on a narrow range of subjects related to the site. Homer had always worked in series, exploring the nuances of a subject through a succession of formal and thematic variations—for example in the group of oils and wood engravings on croquet in the late 1860s. However, the serial nature of his work became even more pronounced after he took up watercolor, because in this quick, impulsive medium he could produce a large group of finished works in a relatively short period of time. Further, while there had previously been only a loose relationship between the oils and wood engravings,[1] beginning with the Gloucester work in the summer of 1873 and continuing until Homer abruptly ended his graphic work the following year, there was a close formal connection between watercolors, oils, and prints of a given subject. *Boys Wading*, for example, is closely related to the vertical watercolor *A Basket of Clams* (fig. 1), which in turn was combined with the watercolor *The Clambake* (Cleveland Museum of Art), showing a group of boys gathered around a fire on the beach, to create the wood engraving *Seaside Sketches—A Clambake* (fig. 2)

published in *Harper's Weekly* in 1873. When translated into the graphic medium these works became more complex and anecdotal, retaining a certain episodic and disjunctive quality reflective of their creation by addition. This process of variation and synthesis is typical of the Gloucester period and suggests a more experimental

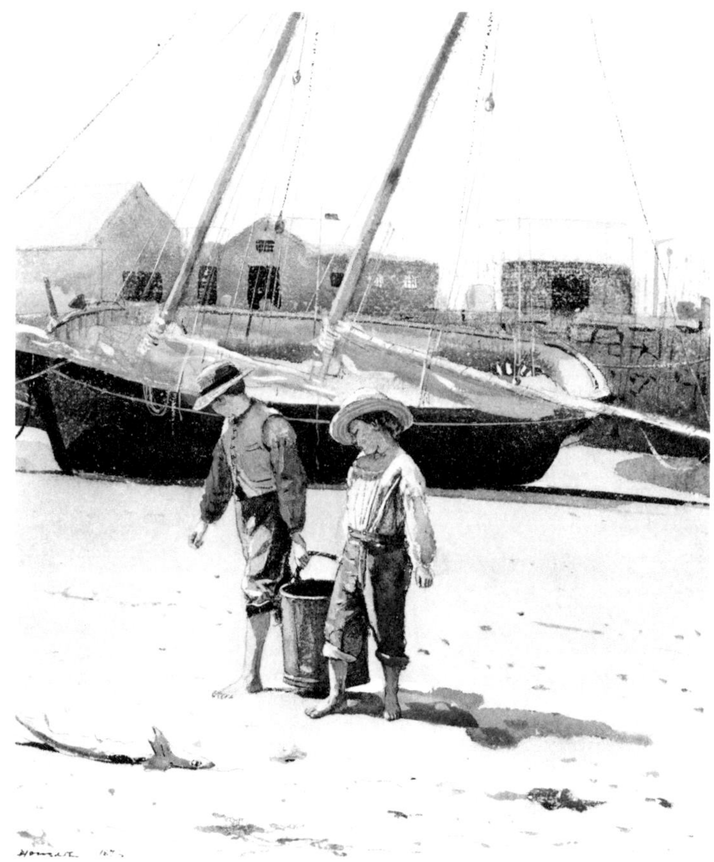

Figure 1. *A Basket of Clams*, 1873. Watercolor, 29.2 x 24.8 cm.
Collection of Diana and Arthur G. Altschul.

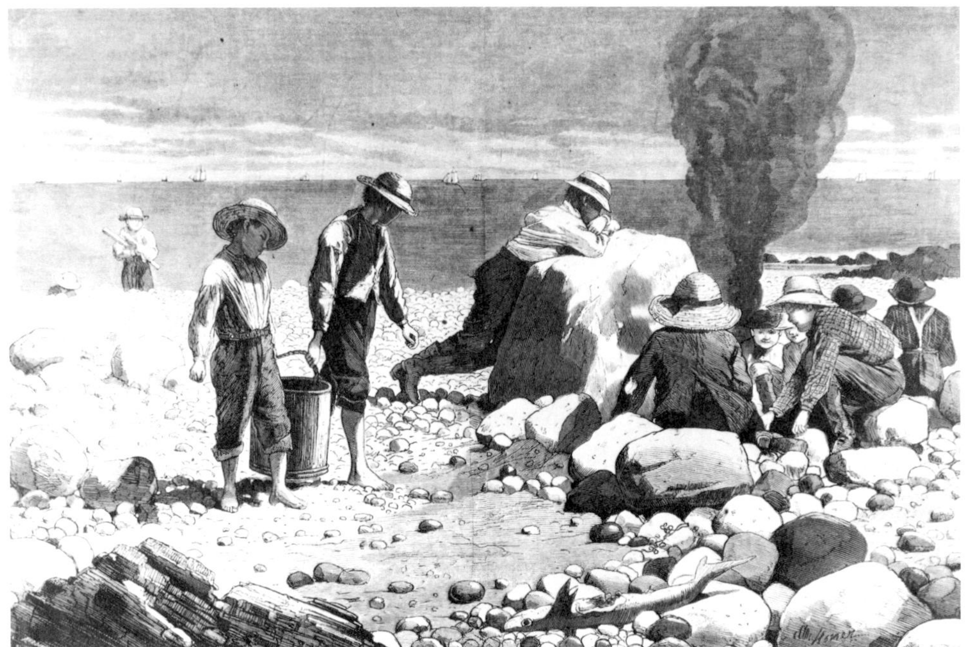

Figure 2. *Seaside Sketches—A Clambake*, 1873. Wood engraving, 23.5 x 35.6 cm. Graphic Arts Collection, Firestone Library, Princeton University.

attitude and greater care on the part of the artist in trying to bring the formal and thematic content of his material to its perfect expression.

Many of the Gloucester works are meticulously composed. Homer particularly liked to play groups of children off against a like number of inanimate objects. In both *A Basket of Clams* and *Boys Wading*, for example, the two youths appear before the twin masts of a ship and a pair of gabled buildings with dark, open doors. The theme of pairs is further reinforced in *Boys Wading* by the two cranes in the upper right corner. The same technique is used to unify the final version of *Breezing Up (A Fair Wind)* of a few years later, in which four boys are set against the four sails of a ship on the horizon.[2] This intricate play between foreground and background is characteristic of Homer's works of the seventies, often

contributing to their meaning while giving them unity.

Formal strength is paralleled by coloristic brilliance and daring experimentation in what was for Homer a new medium. His use of watercolor in the summer of 1873 may have been inspired by the large international exhibition organized by the American Society of Painters in Water Colors, held at the National Academy of Design in New York earlier that year; but, while most contemporary work emphasized a meticulously detailed finish and unified tonal harmony, Homer's handling was direct, at times even coarse and brutal, and his color bright and strident in its contrasts. Typical of traditional contemporary watercolors, however, Homer's early works in this medium depend heavily on gouache, or opaque watercolor, to record details and suggest highlights—for example on the sleeve of the boy on the left, or in the sails of the boat in the background—rather than exploiting the white of the paper for this purpose, as the artist did so well in his later works. The shimmering reflections on the water in the foreground, created by dragging a brush loaded with a light opaque pigment over a darker base so that it just catches the peaks of the rough watercolor paper while leaving the hollows unfilled, creates a remarkable, sparkling effect that is enhanced by the resonance between the cool lavenders and blues and the warm ochers. Such color harmonies were remarkably sophisticated for the time and may have been inspired by the same treatise on color, Michel Chevreul's *The Laws of Contrast of Colour* (1859), that was later to inspire the Impressionists and Post-Impressionists in France. Homer had been given a copy of the book in 1860 by his brother, and later referred to it as his "Bible."[3] The technical brilliance and coloristic sophistication of *Boys Wading* are all the more astonishing when one considers that this was one of the very first works the artist created in watercolor.

A few of Homer's Gloucester watercolors were included in exhibitions early in 1874 and in the spring of

1875. It may have been *Boys Wading*, or works like it, crude and bold in their execution even to modern eyes, that inspired Henry James to comment in 1875 that Homer "is almost barbarously simple, and, to our eye, he is horribly ugly; but there is nevertheless something one likes about him."[4] The reviewer for the *New York Tribune* in 1874 commended Homer's originality, saying he has a "manner of his own" that "has sprung from the artist's individual way of looking at Nature, not from his way of looking at some other man's pictures. . . . These ten sketches—mere memorandum blots and exclamation points as they are . . . are so pleasant to look at, we are almost content not to ask Mr. Homer for a finished piece."[5] It was this perceived lack of finish that dampened the praise of contemporary critics, many of whom recognized Homer's originality and truth to experience, while at the same time finding themselves unable to like or commend his work.

Curiously, the brilliance and spontaneity of handling in *Boys Wading* underscore its seriousness and monumentality. This work is certainly about the sparkle of light on water, but specifically, because it captures such fleeting impressions and fixes them on paper, its momentariness becomes timeless. There is, in much of Homer's Gloucester art, a curious poise between time and not-time, between specificity and universality, that also characterizes the luminist painting of Fitz Hugh Lane, Frederic Edwin Church, Martin Johnson Heade, and John Frederick Kensett. Much of the picture's power comes from the contrast between the momentary flash of summer light and the transfixed, meditative attitudes of the two boys. This mood of quietude and emotional reticence is reinforced by a number of devices: the boys are pushed off into the middle distance; they are self absorbed, engaging neither us nor each other, lost in the contemplation of another world, underwater, that is not visible to us; and they are anonymous and generalized—one even turns his back, his face wholly

obscured. All of these devices work to make the figures aloof from us, physically and psychologically.

In Homer's watercolors meaning is often revealed through the juxtaposition of elements in the composition, particularly the apparently arbitrary, but in fact quite intentional juxtaposition of elements in foreground and background. By the 1870s, very little in Homer's compositions is left to accident. In *The Boat Builders* (Indianapolis Museum of Art) the intent behind the intersection of the sail of the toy boat in the boy's hands with that of the real boat on the horizon is confirmed by the presence of the device in the preparatory drawing.[6] Its significance is made more obvious by the related wood engraving, *Shipbuilding, Gloucester Harbor* (fig. 3), in which boys making toy boats in the foreground are juxtaposed with men making a real boat in the background. In both images a visual contrast between the size of

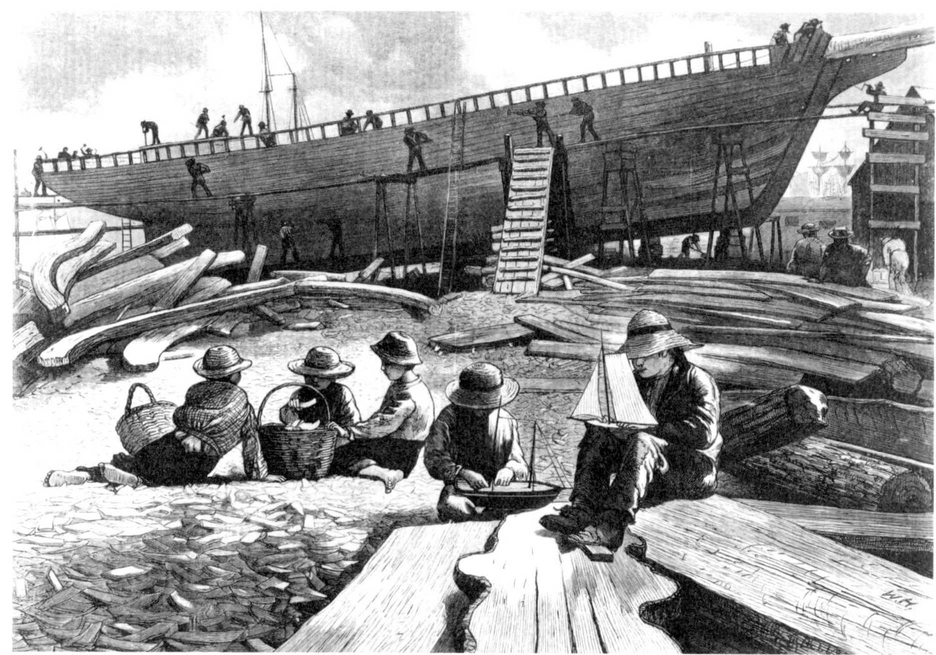

Figure 3. *Shipbuilding, Gloucester Harbor*, 1873. Wood engraving, 23.8 x 34.9 cm. Graphic Arts Collection, Firestone Library, Princeton University.

boats near and far underscores the contrast in meaning between toy boat and real boat. The opposition so pointedly drawn here, of boy's play prefiguring man's work, is a recurrent theme in the paintings and graphics of these years.

While *Boys Wading* appears to be little more than a gentle reverie of summer play, its pendant, *A Basket of Clams*, shows boys at work, and in the corresponding wood engraving the youthful figures are gathered around a fire baking the food they have collected. If not for the clams, would they have anything to eat? Are these in fact images of play or work, of fun or dire necessity? In the case of *Boys Wading*, the answer is obscured by an essential ambiguity of what is happening. Though the boys are placed in opposition to the world of men's work, as in the engraving of *Shipbuilding, Gloucester Harbor*, their play does not anticipate the work that is suggested by the fishing boats in the background. Wading is not a way to catch fish, nor is it a way to collect clams. In *Boys Wading*, a basic ambiguity of action underlies what seems at first to be an obvious and optimistic scene, and this ambiguity is underscored by the boys' distance and anonymity.

In Homer's early Gloucester works there are already hints of the theme of man's mortality, so evident in the artist's later work.[7] In this regard it is significant that at Gloucester Homer first addressed the tenuous connection between the sea and those who depend on it for their living, though more subtly and less directly than in the works of Tynemouth, England, and Prout's Neck, Maine, in which the sea becomes the principal locus of the artist's tragic vision.

In *Boys Wading*, as in *Dad's Coming* (collection of Mr. and Mrs. Paul Mellon), the cranes in the upper right corner suggest gallows,[8] and in *Boys Wading* the dark gaping holes of the barn doors and the white-shrouded ship in the background perhaps allude to the mortality of the boys in the foreground. While this symbolic reading may be stretching the point, these hints of mortality are underscored in the foreground of *A Basket of Clams* by a prominent and grotesque dead fish, which appears again in the wood engraving. (Even in *Boys Wading*, what may be a large clam shell lies on the beach in the center foreground.) Yet why do the boys in *A Basket of Clams* avert their gazes so that their profiles and emotions are obscured, as if to avoid seeing this symbol of life's transience?[9]

In the Gloucester works, intimations of hard work and the uncertainty of existence are concealed within apparently idyllic images of childhood. Many of these scenes of children at play can be read on one level as *memento mori*, and in this regard are connected with the ages-old artistic theme of death's presence even in Arcadia, a tragic vision that Homer may have acquired through his experience of the Civil War.

R.W.

1. A notable exception is *The Army of the Potomac—A Sharpshooter on Picket Duty*, which was closely based on one of the artist's first oils.

2. John Wilmerding observed the general principle and analyzed both *Boys Wading* and *A Basket of Clams* in these terms; see John Wilmerding, *Winslow Homer* (New York, 1972), 88, 90–91. Barbara Novak, *American Painting of the Nineteenth Century* (1969; reprint, New York, 1979), 180, has noted a "strong tendency toward classic organization" in Homer's works of 1873–74.

3. Gordon Hendricks, *The Life and Work of Winslow Homer* (New York, 1979), 157; and Helen A. Cooper, *Winslow Homer Watercolors*, exhib. cat., National Gallery of Art, Amon Carter Museum, Yale University Art Gallery (Washington, D.C., 1986), 28–29. Chevreul's book, *De la loi du contraste simultané des couleurs* (Paris, 1839), was first published in English in 1854; Homer owned the 1859 English edition.

4. Henry James, "On Some Pictures Lately Exhibited," *Galaxy* 20 (July 1875), 93; quoted by Lloyd Goodrich, *Winslow Homer* (New York, 1944), 53.

5. *New York Tribune*, February 14, 1874, 7; quoted by Cooper, *Homer Watercolors*, 1986, 24.

6. Reproduced in Hendricks, *Winslow Homer*, 97.

7. The importance of Homer's tragic vision, particularly in his later works, was first pointed out by Henry Adams in his "Mortal Themes: Winslow Homer," *Art in America* 71 (February 1983), 112–26.

8. John Wilmerding, "Winslow Homer's *Dad's Coming*," in *Essays in Honor of Paul Mellon, Collector and Benefactor*, ed. John Wilmerding (Washington, D.C., 1986), 400.

9. Such harbingers of death recur in the foreground of Homer's images of the shore throughout the 1870s. In her analysis of *Moonlight* (Canajoharie Library and Art Gallery), a curious, sexually charged nocturne showing a man and woman sitting on the shore before a surging sea, Cooper, *Homer Watercolors*, 47, notes the meaningful parallel of foreground details and background action: "the figures' ghostly shadows and the black, skeletonlike seaweed lying in the foreground seem to foretell the death of this relationship." Dead seaweed appears in both the oil and engraved versions of *Dad's Coming*; and a conch shell replaces the agitated dog in the engraved version of *High Tide* (1870). The most peculiar and enigmatic of these images is the engraving *The Wreck of the "Atlantic"—Cast Up by the Sea* (1873), which shows the moment when an old fisherman comes upon the corpse of a voluptuous, classically sculpturesque woman in clinging draperies, lying peacefully on the beach. Curiously, even in such a dramatic moment, Homer shows the man with his gaze averted, his reaction inscrutable.

5. *The Flirt*, 1874

Oil on panel, 20.6 x 31.4 cm. (8⅛ x 12⅜ in.)
Signed lower left: *HOMER*
Private collection

Apparently Homer didn't think highly of *Breezing Up (A Fair Wind)* (fig. 1), now perhaps his most popular work.[1] Although critics hailed this "bold and free picture, excellent in composition, original in conception, admirable in drawing"[2] upon its display at the National Academy exhibition in 1876, Homer discouraged Lawson Valentine, one of the painting's many admirers, from buying the work. The artist believed the listed price of $850 was too high for this valued patron. He wrote to Valentine:

I am very much obliged to you for noticing my picture at the Academy and expressing a wish to buy it. Take my advice and don't do it. I am about to paint much better pictures & will give you a chance at them. If the "Fair Wind" comes home to me from the Academy I shall be glad to sell it to you at a reduced price.[3]

Valentine did not purchase the work, but he did eventually acquire the painting's oil study, *The Flirt*. As such, *The Flirt* bears some relation to the pencil-and-wash *Sketch for "The Bright Side" and "Army Teamsters"* (cat. no.

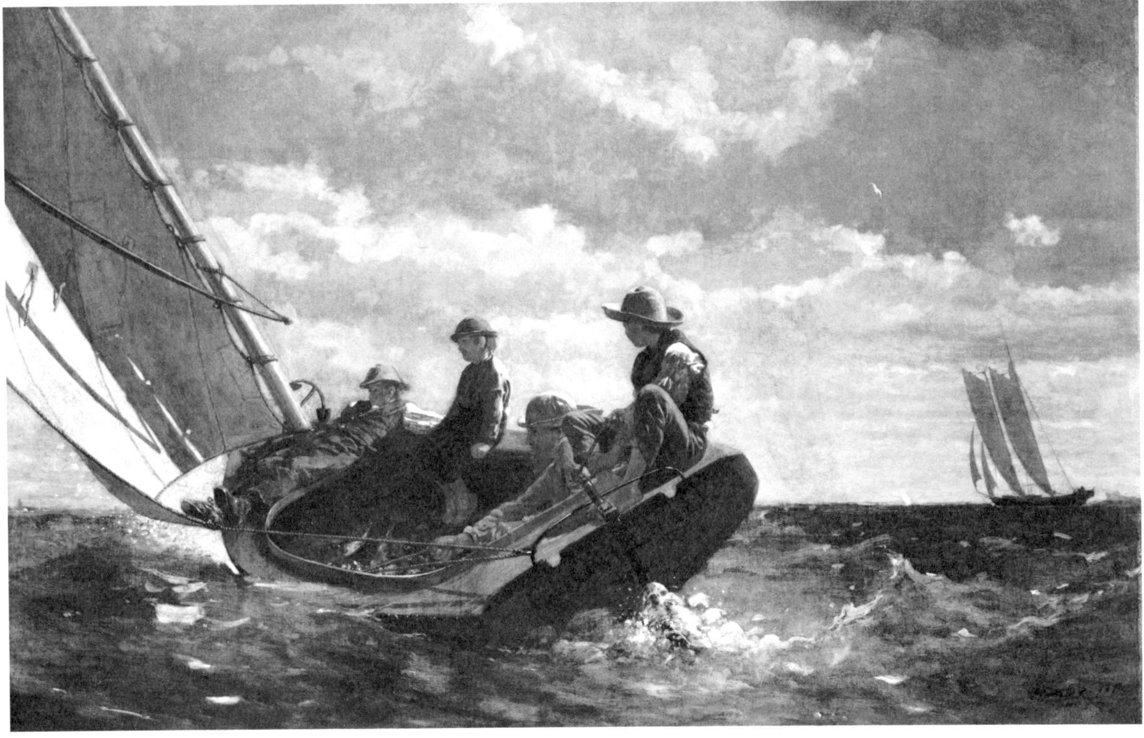

Figure 1. *Breezing Up (A Fair Wind)*, 1876. Oil on canvas, 61.5 x 97 cm. National Gallery of Art, Washington, D.C., gift of the W. L. and May T. Mellon Foundation.

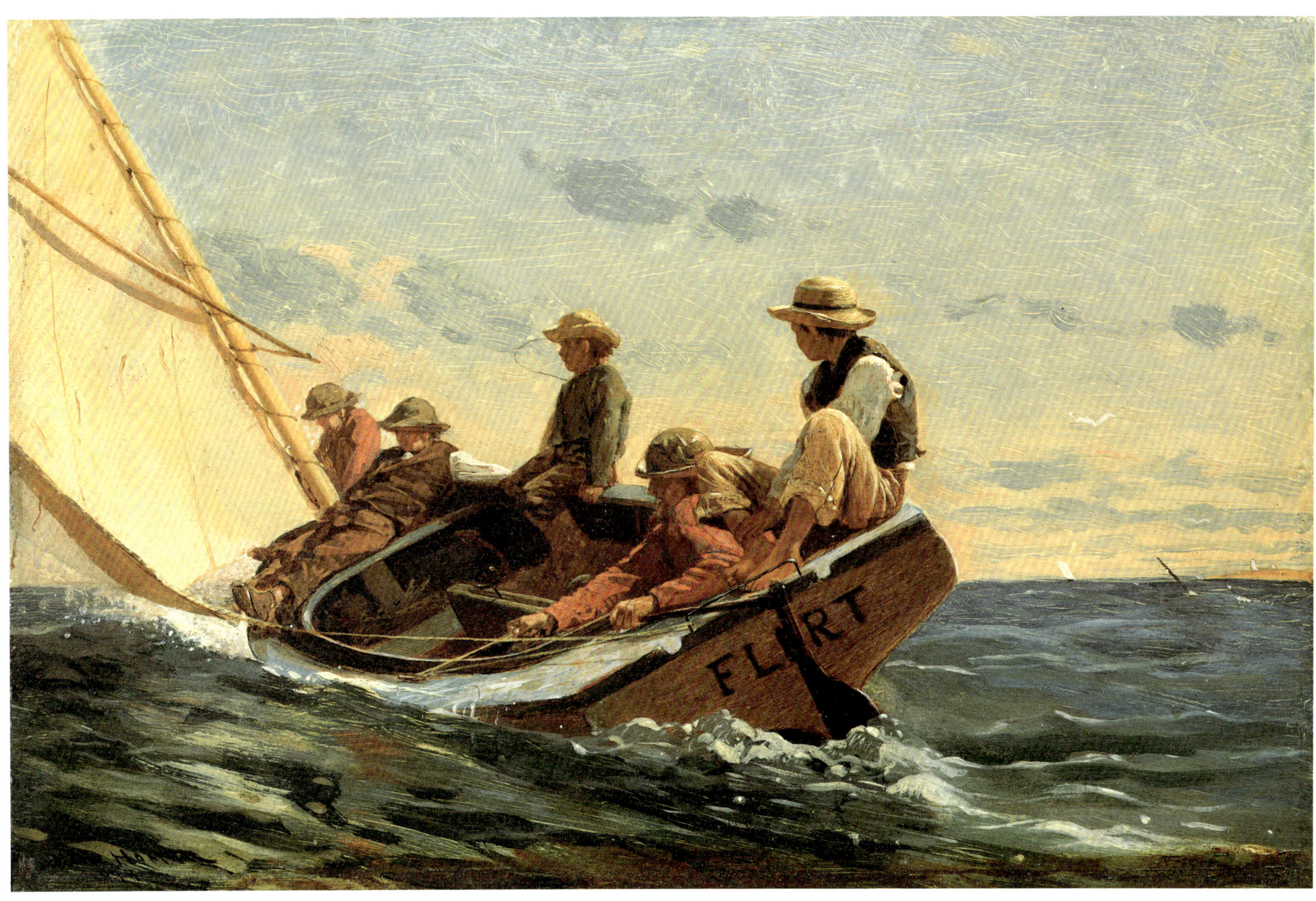
FLIRT

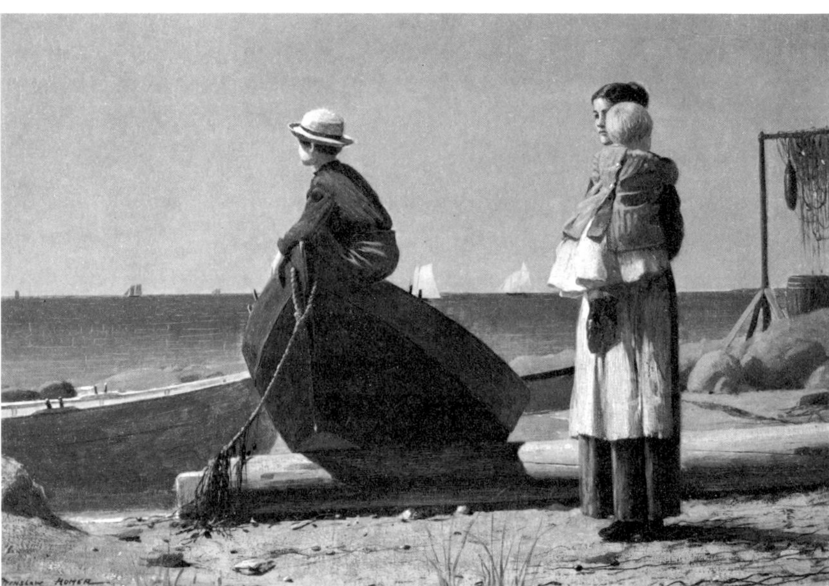

Figure 2. *Dad's Coming (Waiting for Dad)*, 1873. Oil on panel, 22.9 x 34.9 cm. Collection of Mr. and Mrs. Paul Mellon, Upperville, Virginia.

1), since both these preparatory studies served Valentine as substitutes for desired paintings. Like the two little-known Civil War images, *The Flirt* has itself been misunderstood, even suffering the appellation of "a spin-off,"[4] although the small panel is clearly a stage earlier than the final canvas. *The Flirt* can serve as a touchstone for Homer's compositional strategies and thematic interests in the 1870s; it can also address what accounts for the enduring appeal of *Breezing Up*, an American icon. But first it must be understood as part of the artist's creative process.

Beginning in the 1870s, the theme of the sea was never far from Homer's work. In the summer of 1873, as he began serious work in watercolors at Gloucester, Homer became particularly absorbed by the subject of boys and boats, producing such eloquent pictures as *Boys Wading* (cat. no. 4).[5] In many of the images, such as *Dad's Coming* of 1873 (fig. 2), he depicted figures, either solitary or in groups, in isolated poses, lured by

the stark presence of the sea.[6] He employed types—like the poised and expectant boy with wide-brimmed hat in *Dad's Coming*—to build a vocabulary for his seaside and sailing scenes.[7]

Before *Breezing Up*, Homer painted an airy watercolor, *Sailing the Catboat* (fig. 3), probably 1873, in which he peopled the vessel with four boys and added a bearded man at the helm. As in the *Army Teamster* series, he introduced few changes in the composition between the initial watercolor and the finished oil—another indication of his artistic confidence. At this initial stage, he explored the broad masses and motions of the composition, taking advantage of the singular properties of watercolor. By the time he painted *Sailing the Catboat* he had already decided upon the angle of the boat, the approximate positions of its crew, and the novel idea in American painting of allowing the picture's border to truncate the billowing sail.[8] He did not neglect certain details at this stage, composing the shapes of the hats and the two depressions in the transom.

The development of further details, however, required a new medium. Keeping the dimensions of the image roughly the same, Homer switched to oil for *The Flirt*, using his surer touch in this medium to add such fine elements as the rigging, the folds in the clothing, and a name on the boat's stern. Clouds and waves, only suggested in the watercolor, were given precise and modeled form. The artist also eliminated the promontory (probably Gloucester) at the right, setting the scene free from the pull of the mainland. Yet, on the whole, the composition of *Sailing the Catboat* was confirmed rather than changed.

Final amendments refined the image. For *Breezing Up*, Homer made minor changes—such as the colors of the hats—and dramatic ones—such as the appearance of the sky. He rendered sunlight and shadow with greater precision, taking special care with the play of light on the sail and the heads of the boat's passengers. He elimi-

nated the poorly drawn boy in red who had been slouch-
ing at the prow—in *Sailing the Catboat* and *The Flirt* this
lumpy figure appeared ready to slide overboard. Homer
corrected this deficiency with a more visually stable object—an anchor. At the stern, he now entrusted the tiller
to the perched boy. For the boat's title, he replaced the
coy "Flirt" with the more staid "Gloucester," in the process making the name of the vessel less legible. This
change of nomenclature remedied his earlier decision in
The Flirt to delete the distant point of the shore; the
renaming replaced the physical presence of Gloucester with a textual one. As if to give more purpose to
the day's outing, the artist filled the hold of the boat
with fish.

In painting *Breezing Up*, Homer originally added a
vessel close-hauled behind the catboat's stern, but he
changed his mind, instead placing a schooner in the distance. As the pigments have aged, his earlier intention
has reappeared as a shadowy *pentimento*. This process of
revision and correction found in the *Breezing Up* series,
and Homer's ease in different media, were common characteristics of the artist's work in the 1870s.[9]

Homer evidently wished to take his subject one step
further, and present it as a wood engraving. Around
1879 he copied the painting in a drawing of pencil,
crayon, and chalk, preparing the image for an engraver
by simplifying its elements (fig. 4).[10] Although the
abridgment that the drawing presents seems to contra-
dict the sprightly balance of the painting, the drawing
itself answers the limitations demanded by the engraving
medium, including "a stronger emphasis upon outline
than specific detail, continuous line contours and a generalized tonality within the forms."[11] Homer's experience as a graphic illustrator had given him an understanding of the engraver's requirements.

In a similar way, the respective properties of watercolor and oil help account for the differences in spirit in
the works of the *Breezing Up* series. Helen Cooper writes

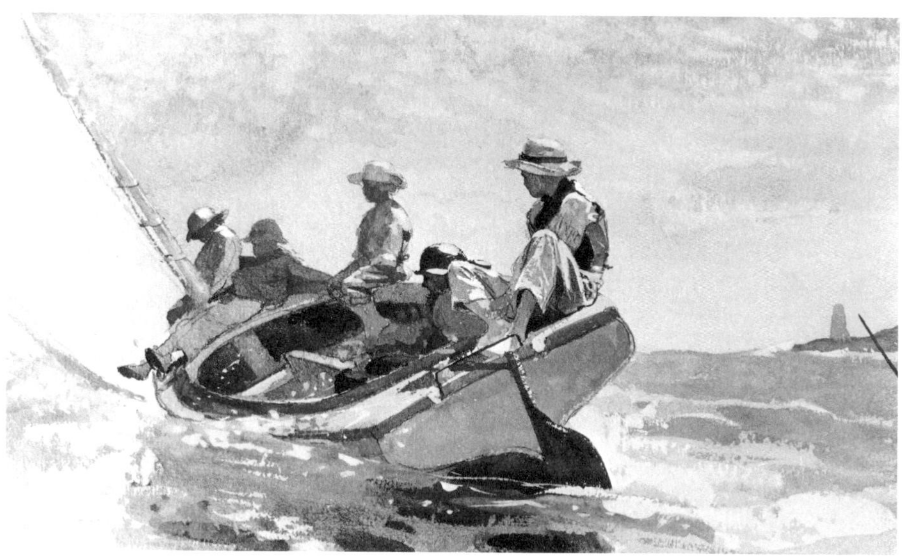

Figure 3. *Sailing the Catboat*, ca. 1873. Watercolor, 24.1 x 34 cm. Private collection.

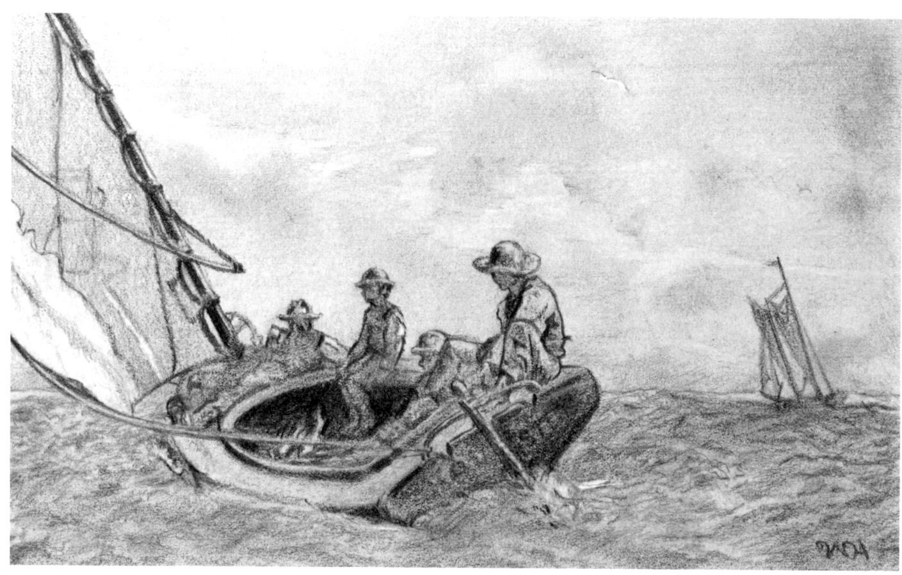

Figure 4. *Breezing Up*, 1879. Graphite, crayon, and chalk, 24 x 33.5 cm. National Gallery
of Art, Washington, D.C., John Davis Hatch Collection; Avalon Fund.

47

that the "very fluid and transparent character" of water-color makes it an appropriate medium for effects of motion. In the case of *Sailing the Catboat*, "the gesture of the brush itself suggests the light, quick movement of the boat as it skims across the water."[12] On the other hand, the oil technique, shared by *Breezing Up* and *The Flirt*, gains in detail and modeling what it loses in immediacy. According to Cooper, *Sailing the Catboat* differs from *Breezing Up* in both technique and intention: "The watercolor recreates the spontaneous experience; the oil sums up the idea."[13] *The Flirt*, as an oil sketch, fits somewhere in between.

Although Homer's sensitivity to the properties of each medium mark the stages of the *Breezing Up* sequence, it is the striking composition of the subject that makes the image so memorable. As an intermediate step, *The Flirt* concisely reveals the vigor of Homer's conception. The painting's border cuts off much of the sail, aiding the illusion of speed. The close viewpoint, with the boat itself turning away and pitched at a steep angle, seems even more startling in a picture so small. The forceful diagonals of hull and sail play with the right angles suggested by the upright boys, who sit perpendicular to the strong line of the horizon. These formal devices work together to make the catboat seem ready to sail off the picture surface.

This remarkable compositional strategy reflects the potent influence of Japanese art upon Homer's work, even at this early date. Albert Ten Eyck Gardner has argued that Homer's 1866 trip to Paris was "the most important event in his entire career as an artist," because it gave him the opportunity to observe Japanese decorative arts and prints, either in the shops of importers or in the studios of French artists.[14] More recently, some scholars have proposed that Japanese influence most likely only confirmed compositional tendencies already present in Homer's work.[15] Images like *The Flirt* certainly exhibit what Barbara Novak has termed "the

Japanese predilection for abrupt diagonal perspectives" found frequently in Homer's oeuvre.[16]

The lasting appeal of *Breezing Up*, however, is not just in its striking composition. Since the painting was first exhibited, viewers have responded to its symbolic meanings and its mood, which seem as compelling today as they must have seemed over a century ago. In its sheer optimism, *Breezing Up* and its predecessors present a departure from many of Homer's seaside images of the 1870s. In works like *Dad's Coming*, the sea represents an enigma, or more darkly, a menacing yet indeterminate threat. Other boating images, such as the engraving *Shipbuilding, Gloucester Harbor* (Firestone Library, Princeton University), also from 1873, juxtapose the worlds of men and boys, where the mature creations of the former dwarf the childish attempts of the latter. By contrast, in *The Flirt* and *Breezing Up*, the worlds of young and old are in proportion, much like the delicate balance achieved by the sailboat itself in the stiff breeze. The equilibrium of forces present in sailing implies a harmony between nature and humankind. In *The Flirt*, an older man holds the tiller; in *Breezing Up*, Homer consigned the tiller to the boy at the stern. This transfer of skills from an older to a younger generation may also indicate the passage of time.

Perhaps the harmony of old and new grew from a sense of optimism, or, more accurately, nostalgia, current in the 1870s. The traumatic period of Civil War and Reconstruction plunged Americans into unprecedented and wrenching change. Observers felt they had witnessed a nation forced into maturity. A Harvard professor writing in 1869 judged that the war produced a "great gulf between what happened before in our century and what has happened since, or what is likely to happen hereafter."[17] *Breezing Up*, painted in the centennial year of 1876, portrays an image of America having survived the turning point; it shows a nation simultaneously conscious of its youth and new-found maturity.

Such a reading is not inconsistent with the surface meaning of the blithe boating scene, which surely addresses the relationship between old and young. Youth is a relative concept, but nostalgia for youth only comes with maturity. Homer's knowing celebration of the fun of boyhood, codified in his study *The Flirt*, is the final ingredient in the appeal of *Breezing Up*.

F.I.

1. For the present popularity of this work see, for example, Gordon Hendricks, *The Life and Work of Winslow Homer* (New York, 1979), 118–19.
2. "Exhibition of the National Academy," *New York Times*, April 8, 1876, 6. Although not unreserved in his admiration, the critic thought two of Homer's five pictures in the exhibition were of "very high merit," and of these two, "A Fair Wind" (the title under which Homer exhibited the painting) was "perhaps the better one," adding that the "drawing is simply superb."
3. Homer to Lawson Valentine, April 3, 1876, Harold T. Pulsifer Papers, Special Collections, Colby College, Waterville, Maine; in Hendricks, *Winslow Homer*, 119.
4. Hendricks, *Winslow Homer*, caption to fig. 174.
5. See, in addition, Helen A. Cooper, *Winslow Homer Watercolors*, exhib. cat., National Gallery of Art, Amon Carter Museum, Yale University Art Gallery (Washington, D.C., 1986), figs. 5, 6, 9, 10, 11, 23–28.
6. For this group, see, in particular, John Wilmerding, "Winslow Homer's *Dad's Coming*," in *Essays in Honor of Paul Mellon, Collector and Benefactor*, ed. John Wilmerding (Washington, D.C., 1986), 388–401.
7. See Cooper, *Homer Watercolors*, figs. 9–12, 23–26. Many of these boys are seated, as in the *Breezing Up* series.
8. Two oils of 1874, Thomas Eakins's *Sailing* (Philadelphia Museum of Art), and Edouard Manet's *Boating* (The Metropolitan Museum of Art), provide contemporary examples of this new compositional practice.
9. Philip C. Beam, *Winslow Homer Watercolors*, exhib. cat., Bowdoin College Museum of Art (Brunswick, Maine, 1983), 19.
10. Gary Burger has described this drawing in detail in Gary Burger and John Wilmerding, *100 American Drawings: Loan Exhibition from the Collection of John Davis Hatch*, exhib. cat., Heim Gallery (London, 1976), no. 67, pl. 69.
11. Ibid., no. 67.
12. Cooper, *Homer Watercolors*, 38.
13. Ibid., 38.
14. Albert Ten Eyck Gardner, *Winslow Homer, American Artist: His World and Work* (New York, 1961), 93.
15. Sally Mills, ed., *Japanese Influences in American Art 1853–1900*, exhib. cat., Sterling and Francine Clark Art Institute (Williamstown, Mass., 1981), 18–20. Barbara Novak, *American Painting of the Nineteenth Century* (New York, 1979), 166–67.
16. Novak, *American Painting*, 166.
17. George Ticknor in James M. McPherson, *Battle Cry of Freedom* (New York, 1988), 861.

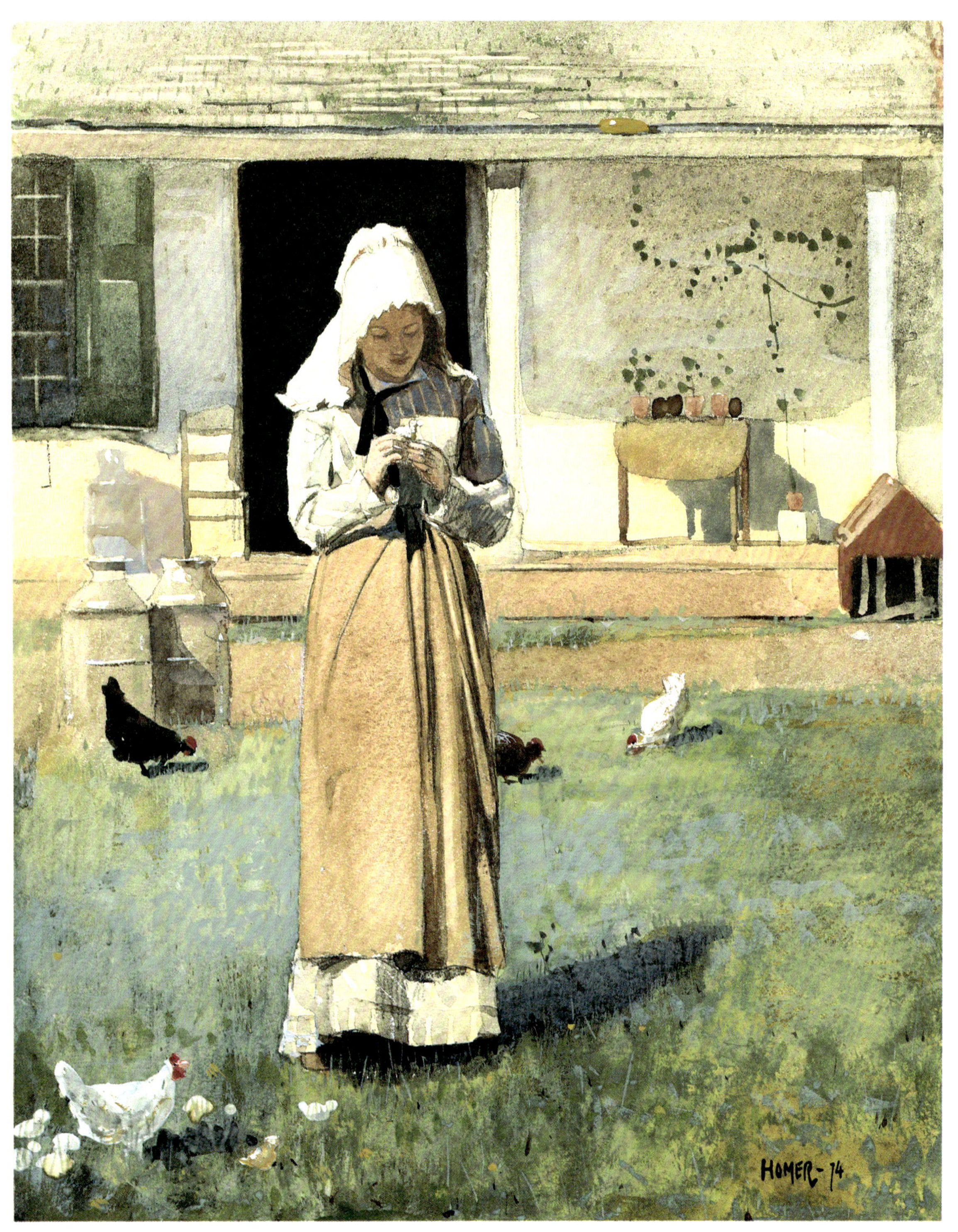
HOMER - 74

6. *A Sick Chicken*, 1874

Watercolor, graphite, and gouache, 24.8 x 19.7 cm. (9¾ x 7¾ in.)
Signed and dated lower right: *HOMER—74*
Private collection

Homer's watercolor *A Sick Chicken* was painted in 1874, probably at Lawson Valentine's summer home in Walden, New York.[1] It is closely related in theme and format to two other watercolors of that year, *Fresh Eggs* and *Hunting for Eggs* (figs. 1, 2). Like *Berry Pickers* and *Boys Wading* (cat. nos. 3, 4), *A Sick Chicken* was painted during the period in which Homer was relinquishing his career as a graphic artist for the life of an independent painter.

Homer's training as an illustrator left an indelible stamp upon his mature style. The limitations of the wood-engraving medium required that he compose his works in distinct tonal masses, balancing light against dark and line against form. This concern carried over

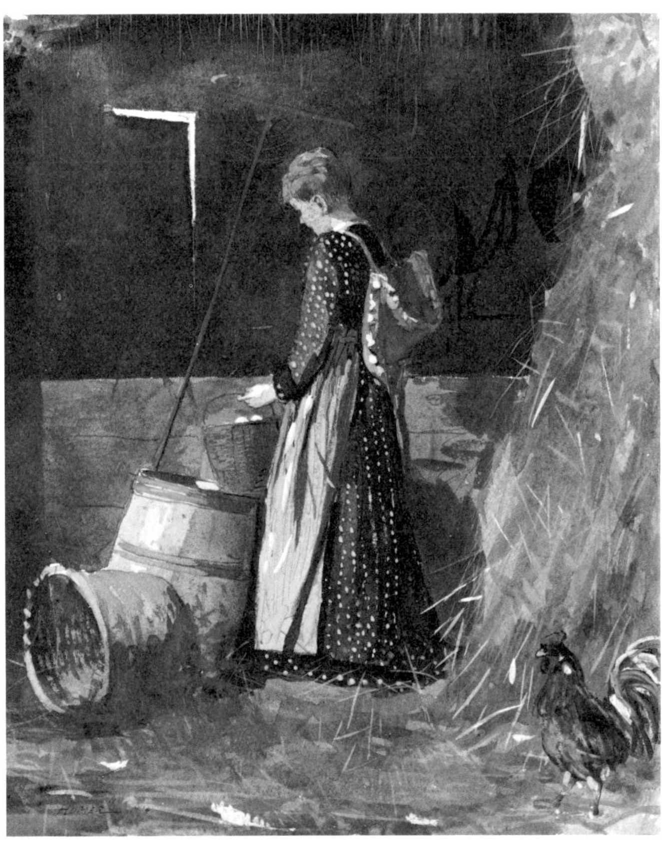

Figure 1. *Fresh Eggs*, 1874. Watercolor, graphite, and gouache, 23.5 x 19.1 cm. (sight). Collection of Mr. and Mrs. Paul Mellon, Upperville, Virginia.

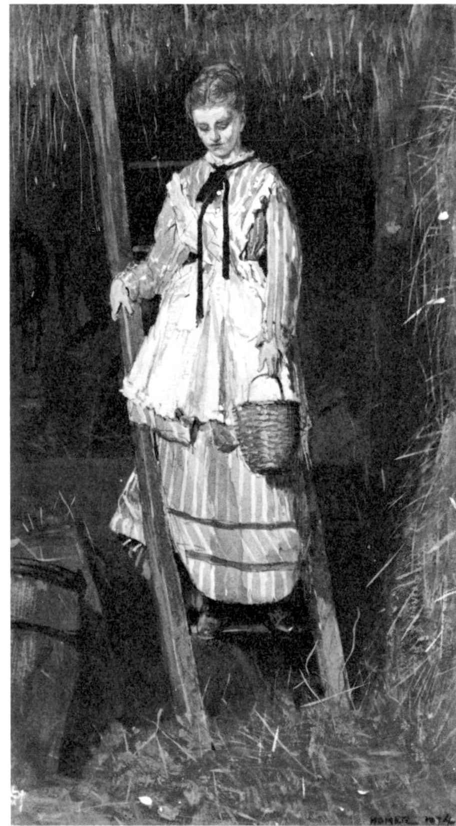

Figure 2. *Hunting for Eggs*, 1874. Gouache over graphite, 24.8 x 14 cm. Sterling and Francine Clark Art Institute, Williamstown, Massachusetts.

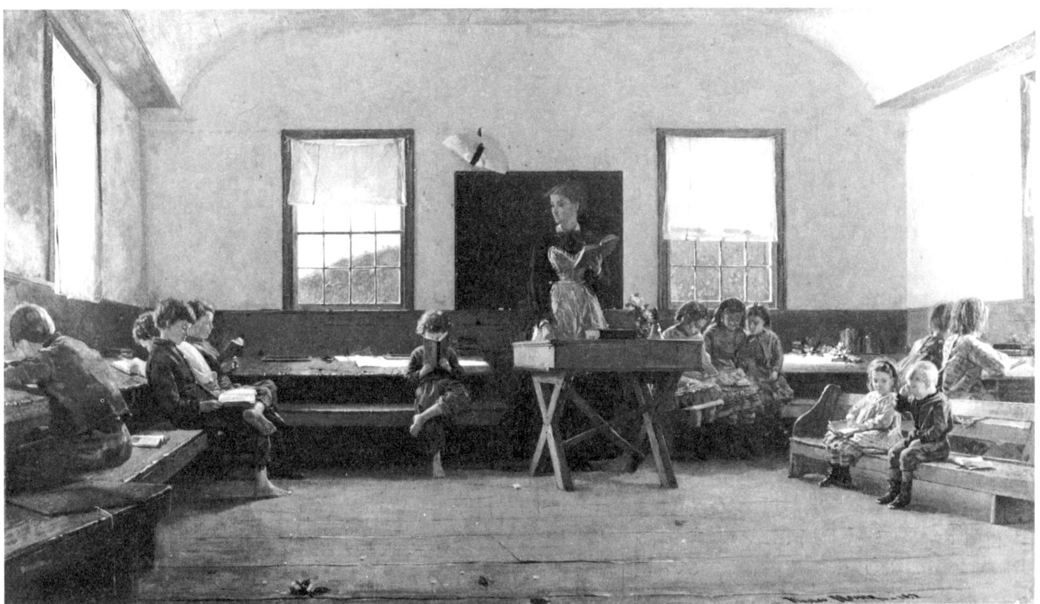

Figure 3. *The Country School*, 1871. Oil on canvas, 54.3 x 97.5 cm. The Saint Louis Art Museum.

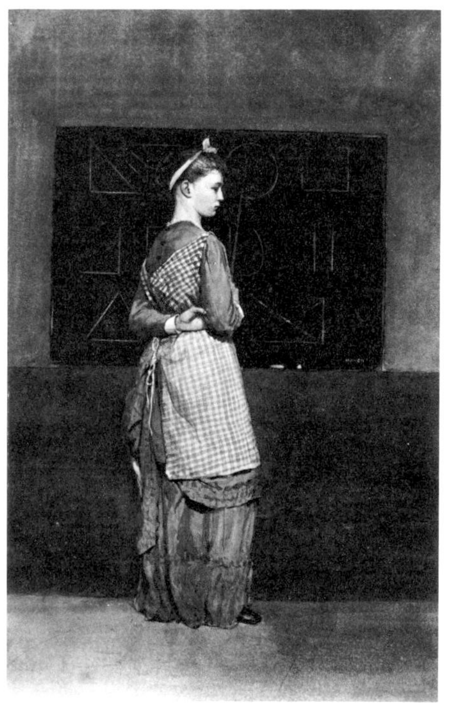

Figure 4. *The Blackboard*, 1877. Watercolor, 48.3 x 30.8 cm. (sight). Collection of Jo Ann and Julian Ganz.

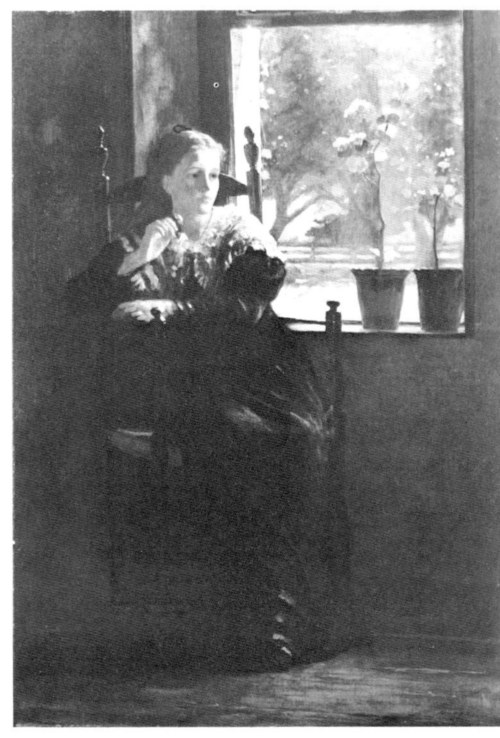

Figure 5. *At the Window*, 1892. Oil on canvas, 57.4 x 40 cm. The Art Museum, Princeton University, gift of Francis Bosak, Class of 1931, and Mrs. Bosak.

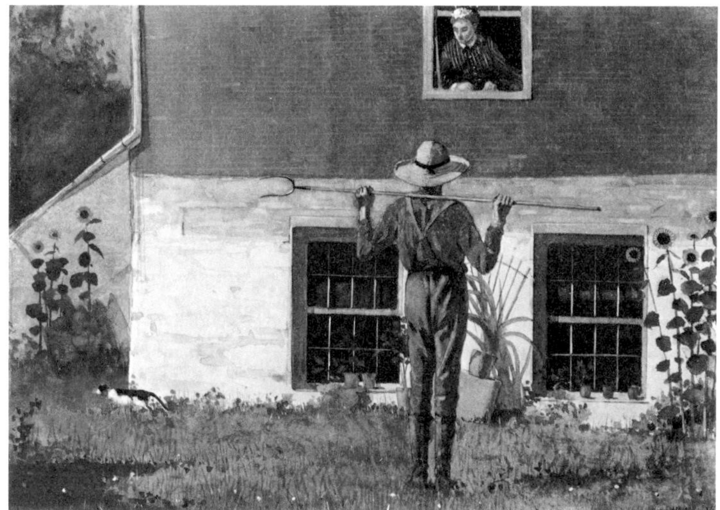

Figure 6. *Rustic Courtship*, 1874. Watercolor and gouache, 21.9 x 31.1 cm. Collection of Mr. and Mrs. Paul Mellon, Upperville, Virginia.

into his painted works: "I have never tried to do anything but get the true relationship of values; that is, the values of dark and light and the values of color," he once said.[2] Although probably not intended for reproduction, *A Sick Chicken* contains one of the most dramatically stark tonal contrasts in Homer's watercolor oeuvre: a brilliant white bonnet set against the impenetrable blackness of a doorway beyond. Critics did not always immediately appreciate the daring Homer displayed in works such as this: "With a little of the flavour to the mental palate of the pickle or perhaps of olives," commented a writer for *The Art Journal*, in a homey analogy, "one may require time to relish it, but when once liked it is heartily enjoyed."[3]

Homer's placement of his female figure against the rigid geometry of a farmyard porch is a characteristic tactic of this period. In addition to similarly planar backdrops in *Fresh Eggs* and *Hunting for Eggs*, we see the same tendency in other figure studies, such as *The Country School* (fig. 3), *The Blackboard* (fig. 4), *At the Window* (fig. 5), and *Rustic Courtship* (fig. 6). Besides justifying Homer's distinct tonal contrasts, the contained space and rectilinear background of these works emphasize the irregular outlines of the female forms and serve to draw attention to the subjects' modest poses.

Homer's artistic attitudes in this decade were predicated upon biographical contrasts, as well: though unmarried, he painted women and children; though established in his New York studio, he painted rustic subjects in rural settings. Whether these choices point to a kind of collective escapism in 1870s America—from urbanization, industrialization, and gruesome memories of the Civil War—or whether they represented objects of personal desire for the artist, we do not know. In either case, the typically detached manner in which Homer renders the girl of *A Sick Chicken* ensures that any untoward affection he might have had for his subject would be sublimated in the work. Indeed, the stillness and self-absorption of the young woman portrayed here—described by one art historian as "an American Hera of Samos"[4]—only increases the distance between the viewer and this scene of nascent maternal instinct. Homer's natural reticence saved the work from excessive sentimentality, while his illustrator's background allowed it to retain a sense of narrative action. *A Sick Chicken*, if only a minor work by Homer, is at least a fully resolved one, and it sustains comparison with any other of his watercolors from this decade for its technical sophistication and thematic interest.

D.N.

1. Gordon Hendricks, *The Life and Work of Winslow Homer* (New York, 1979), 110.
2. Quoted by John W. Beatty, "Recollections of an Intimate Friendship," in Lloyd Goodrich, *Winslow Homer* (New York, 1944), 220.
3. S. N. Carter, "The Water-Colour Exhibition," *The Art Journal*, n.s., 5 (March 1879): 94. Of another watercolor in this exhibition, Carter writes: "It takes an artist as well informed as Mr. Homer to dare to contrast such a dark, clear shadow with the brilliant dash of sunshine which isolates the [figure] from the spectator, and throws her woody retreat into a poetical remoteness."
4. Barbara Novak, *American Painting of the Nineteenth Century* (New York, 1969), 180.

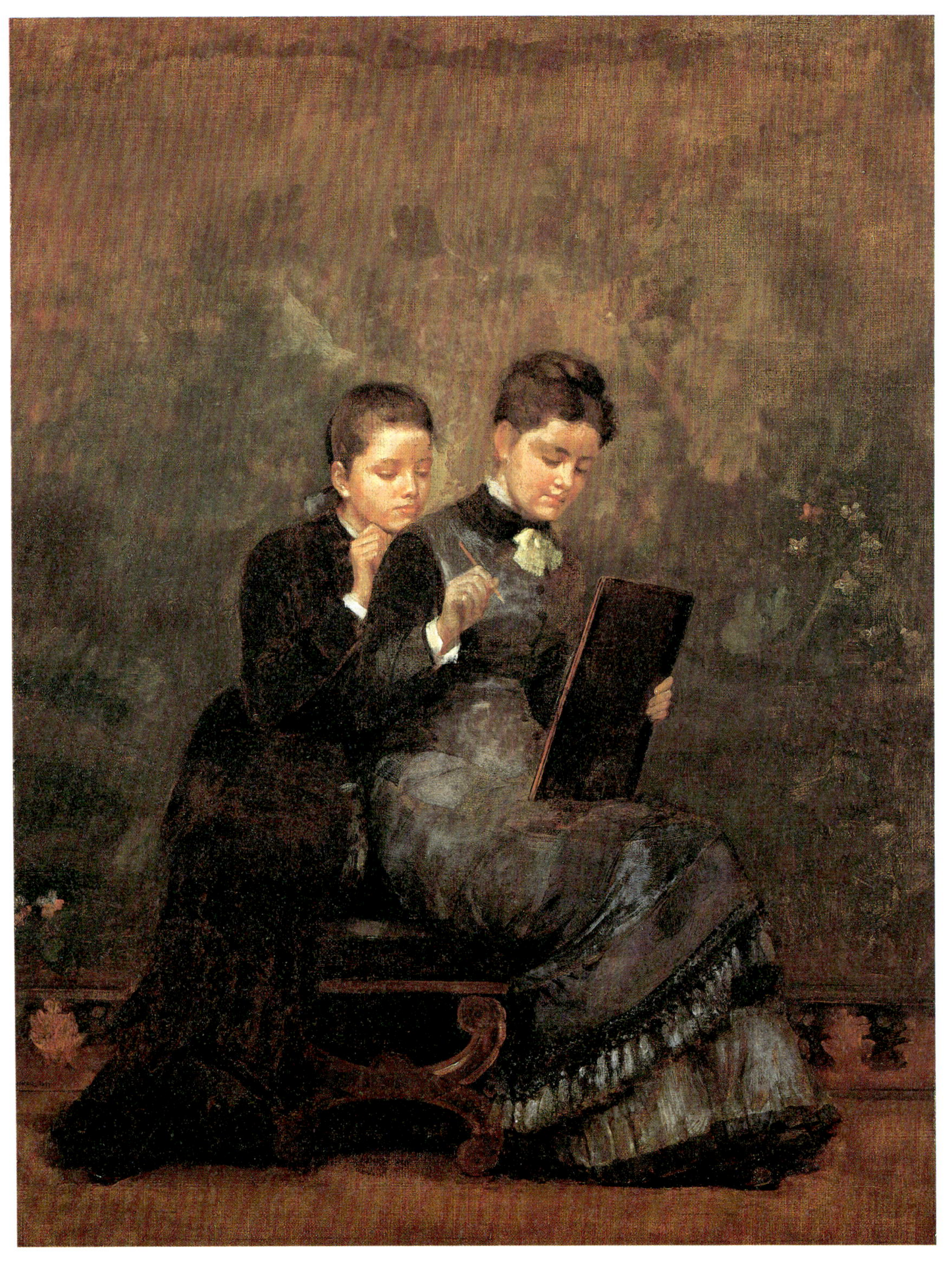

7. *Almira Houghton Valentine and Mary Chamberlain Valentine*, 1877

Oil on canvas, 57.8 x 45 cm. (22¾ x 17¾ in.)
Signed and dated lower left: *HOMER 1877*
Wadsworth Atheneum, Hartford, Connecticut
Gift of the Lawson Valentine Foundation

Winslow Homer painted suprisingly few portraits, considering the overwhelmingly figural emphasis in his work. Most of the portraits of known subjects depict friends or relatives, and these images seem often to have had great personal significance for the artist. The watercolor portrait of his brother Charles Homer, for example, was one of the works Homer had with him in New York after his return from Tynemouth, England. He installed it in a prominent place over the fireplace in the apartment of his cousin, Samuel T. Preston, where it is visible in a contemporary photograph.[1] Homer's portrait of Helena de Kay (fig. 1), a noted flower painter, was inscribed to her on the occasion of her marriage,[2] and *Shall I Tell Your Fortune?* (private collection), said by the artist's family to portray the one love of his life, who married another man, remained in Homer's studio until his death.[3] We can surmise that Homer might not even have painted portraits of the Valentine girls had they not been the daughters of his close friend and patron, Lawson Valentine.[4]

Women were a favorite subject in Homer's art of the 1870s, and his depictions of them undergo a clear evolution from those of the late 1860s, when he shows sociable, active women enjoying the outdoors—playing croquet, hiking, fishing, riding, bathing, and promenading on the shore. In the seventies, his women are typically alone, aloof, and self-absorbed. This emphasis on solitary females begins in the early seventies with the strong, optimistic images of teachers, but by the middle of the decade the women seem more delicate, isolated, and vulnerable. In the early seventies they are almost invariably presented in conjunction with flowers or in a garden, where they appear comfortable in their natural surroundings; in the later seventies, in contrast, particularly in the series of carefully worked monumental watercolors of 1876 to 1877, they are often shown inside, in a rarefied and highly artificial studio setting with a plain background and a few ornate props—a carved stool and table, or a porcelain elephant (fig. 2). When a woman does appear in the garden in these later works, as in *Portrait of a Lady* (collection of Ogden Mills Phipps) and *The Trysting Place* (fig. 3), she seems strangely ill-at-ease and out of place in these surroundings, clothed in an impractical white, flounced dress.

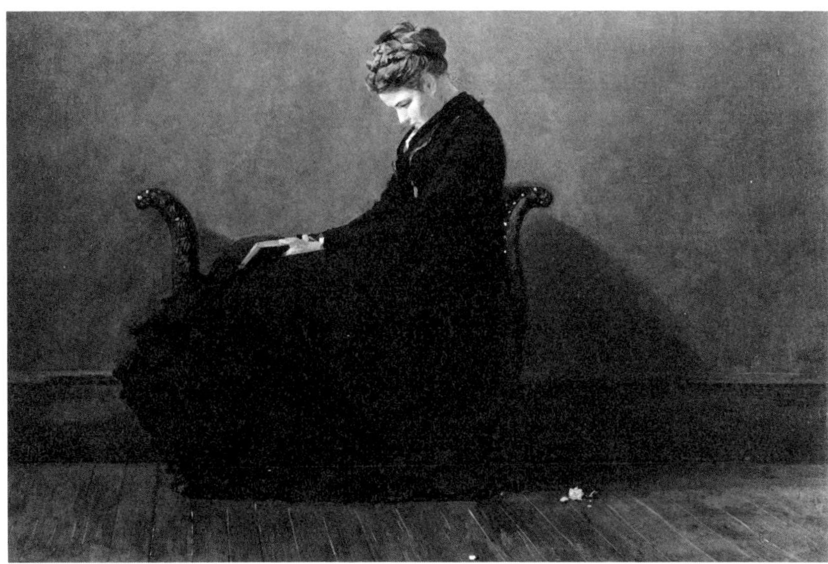

Figure 1. *Portrait of Helena de Kay*, ca. 1873. Oil on panel, 31 x 47 cm. Thyssen-Bornemisza Collection, Lugano, Switzerland.

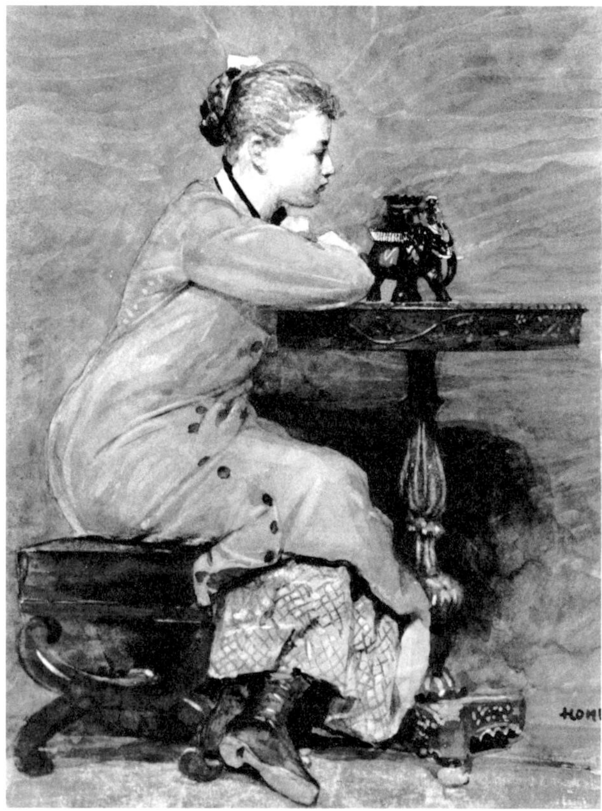

Figure 2. *Woman and Elephant*, ca. 1877. Watercolor, 29.9 x 22.2 cm. Albright-Knox Art Gallery, Buffalo, New York.

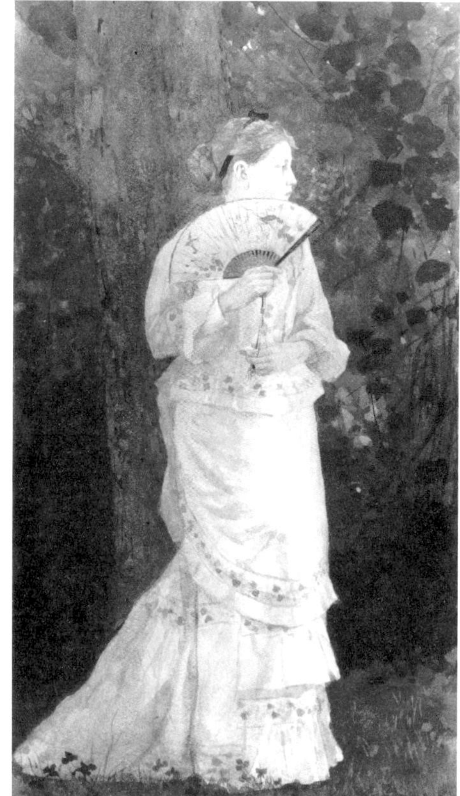

Figure 3. *The Trysting Place*, 1875. Watercolor, 35 x 20.5 cm. Firestone Library, Princeton University, bequest of Laurence Hutton.

In Homer's images of women in the 1870s, the recurring themes of reading and the open window function—as does the garden—as metaphors for entry into an alternate world. These themes may reflect the contemporary Victorian idealization of feminine virtues and particularly the belief that women should be pure and delicate and kept unsullied by the man's world of work and business. Further, the association of women with reading was a common motif in contemporary art and literature in both England and America, because of the popularity of the sentimental novel written by and for women to fill their leisure hours.[5] It is significant that many of Homer's paintings of women in the 1870s are not individual portraits in the true sense. Though they likely were painted from specific models (there has been a great deal of speculation about the possible subjects of these works), they appear to function more as evocations of femininity. Homer consistently generalizes the features of his female sitters, bringing them closer to the type of beauty he had already developed by the late sixties in his images of croquet games and beach life—pure features, large oval eyes, voluptuous figures, fashionable attire, and statuesque bearing.

Homer's portrait of the Valentine girls is consistent

with his other depictions of women in the period, though it is exceptional in showing two identifiable women. Homer was fond of pairs and created a number of works showing two women in a landscape, including *Promenade on the Beach* (1880, Museum of Fine Arts, Springfield, Massachusetts) and *A Summer Night* (1890, Musée d'Orsay), but their pairing in a portrait is unusual and may simply reflect the exigencies of the commission. There is not as strong a mood of emotional isolation and psychological distance in this portrait as in the many contemporary pictures of single women; nevertheless, the gazes of the Valentine sisters are averted, and they

are absorbed, apparently with an artist's sketchbook. Although indoors, the women are shown in conjunction with flowers; however, Homer has placed the figures against an almost neutral background, unusual for his portraits of the early 1870s but characteristic of the group of monumental, carefully finished watercolors created at about the same time in his New York studio. The seated three-quarters profile view of the figure on the right, and even the ornately carved stool the girls sit on reappears in both *Woman Peeling a Lemon* (fig. 4) and *Woman and Elephant*.

The blank background and the seated figure in profile

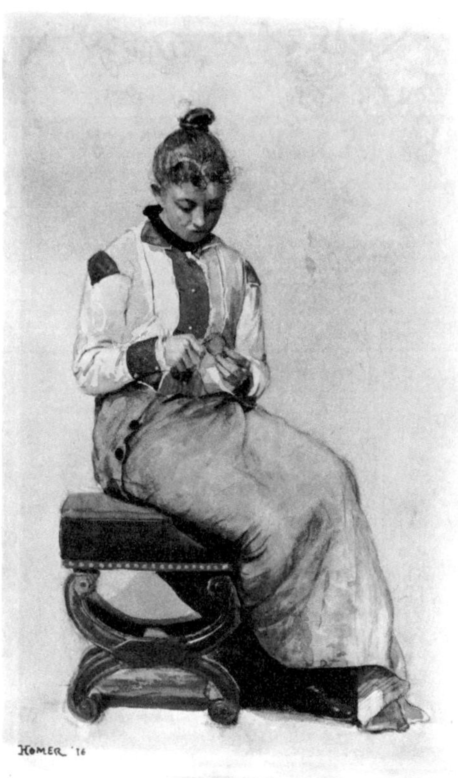

Figure 4. *Woman Peeling a Lemon*. Watercolor over chalk, 47.9 x 30.5 cm. Sterling and Francine Clark Art Institute, Williamstown, Massachusetts.

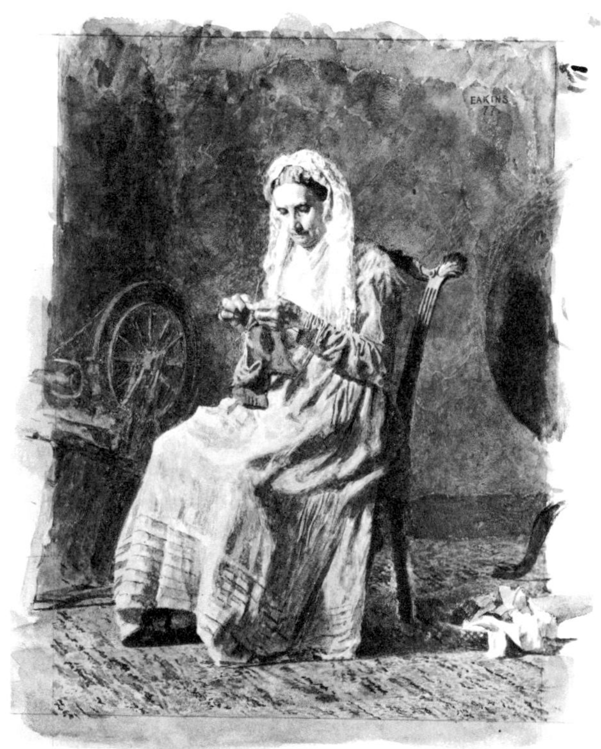

Figure 5. Thomas Eakins (American, 1844–1916), *Seventy Years Ago*, 1877. Watercolor, 39.7 x 27.9 cm. The Art Museum, Princeton University, gift of Mrs. Frank Jewett Mather, Jr.

occur in other Homer works of this period, including the portrait of the artist's brother Charles of 1880 and the watercolor *Girl Seated* (private collection) of 1879. The ultimate expression of this portrait type is the *Portrait of Helena de Kay* of about 1873. The result, in each of these paintings, is an image of iconic simplicity and force. Homer's use of such formal reduction may therefore be tied to the personal significance of the sitter, and in this regard the portrait of the Valentine girls would be no exception, since the artist was a frequent guest in the Valentine household.

These devices have close parallels in the work of other contemporary artists in America, notably the portraits of Thomas Eakins. His genre scene *Seventy Years Ago* (fig. 5) is exactly contemporary with Homer's Valentine portrait and the monumental studio watercolors, and shares with them not only the spare background but also the seated woman in profile absorbed in a task or object, and (as in the watercolors) the careful construction of the work from superimposed layers of transparent pigments. In fact, the old woman in *Seventy Years Ago* bears a striking resemblance to the figure on the right in the Valentine portrait—undoubtedly Almira Valentine—not only in her pose but also in the subtle play of gray and black in the dress. There is an even closer resemblance between Almira and the figure in *Girl Seated*, which was painted two years later than these two works, but likely is another depiction of Lawson's older daughter.

The obvious formal precedent for all of these works, particularly the Eakins watercolor and Homer's *Portrait of Helena de Kay* and *Girl Seated*, is Whistler's *Arrangement in Grey and Black: Portrait of the Painter's Mother* (Musée d'Orsay) of 1871. The composition, though not its coloristic novelty, could have been known to both Homer and Eakins by the wood engraving published in the *Illustrated London News* in June 1872.[6] The radical formal reduction of Whistler's painting (in this case he also portrayed someone who was close to him) seems necessary to explain the extreme simplicity of Homer's portrait of Helena de Kay. However, the formal motifs of the seated figure in profile and the empty background were widely disseminated in French avant-garde art at the time, and without speculating on how Homer might have seen them, it is interesting to note that Degas's *Portrait of the Painter James Tissot* (The Metropolitan Museum of Art) and Manet's *Emile Zola* (Musée d'Orsay), both showing a man in seated profile and both painted in a muted range of tones, were created about the time of Homer's visit to Paris in the later 1860s, while Fantin-Latour's *Portrait of Edouard Manet* (Art Institute of Chicago), showing the painter standing against a radically reduced background reminiscent of Manet's own earlier work, had just been created and was exhibited at the Salon of 1867. The influence of Homer's trip to Paris on his art has always been a vexing and controversial problem in Homer scholarship, but the influence at least of Whistler's *Portrait of the Painter's Mother* seems incontrovertible. Homer's diminutive portrait of the Valentine sisters is typical of his paintings of women in the 1870s, and its formal austerity, for which Whistler set the example, may in fact belie his affection for the sitters.

R.W.

1. Gordon Hendricks, *The Life and Work of Winslow Homer* (New York, 1979), 169.

2. Barbara Novak, *The Thyssen-Bornemisza Collection: Nineteenth-Century American Painting* (London, 1986), 252–53.

3. Lloyd Goodrich, *Winslow Homer* (New York, 1944), 56–57. For further discussion of Homer's mysterious lost love, see Henry Adams "Winslow Homer's Mystery Woman," *Art & Antiques* (November 1984), 38–45; Helen A. Cooper, *Winslow Homer Watercolors*, exhib. cat., National Gallery of Art, Amon Carter Museum, Yale University Art Gallery (Washington, D.C., 1986), 43–44, 51, n. 44.

4. Hendricks, *Winslow Homer*, 137, records that a portrait of Almira (b. 1854) and Mary (b. 1862) was under way early in 1880 and was paid for by June 11 of that year; another was in progress early in 1883. On the basis of the apparent ages of the girls in the present work, however, Hendricks doubted that it was either of these documented commissions and suggested that it was an earlier work of about 1875. The signature and date were recently discovered after the painting was cleaned.

5. Ann Douglas, *The Feminization of American Culture* (New York, 1977), 9; referred to by Cooper, *Homer Watercolors*, 50.

6. A photograph in the Avery collection in the New York Public Library was inscribed to Avery by Whistler in 1872. For the history of the painting, see Andrew McLaren Young, Margaret MacDonald, Robin Spencer, and Hamish Miles, *The Paintings of James McNeill Whistler* (New Haven and London, 1980), no. 101.

8. *On the Fence (On the Farm)*, 1878

Watercolor and gouache over graphite, 28.6 x 22.1 cm.
(11¼ x 8¹¹⁄₁₆ in.)
Signed and dated lower left: *HOMER 1878*
Private collection

9. *On the Stile*, ca. 1878

Watercolor and gouache over graphite, 22 x 28.2 cm.
(8¹¹⁄₁₆ x 11⅛ in.)
Signed lower right: *HOMER*
Private collection

Lawson Valentine acquired Houghton Farm, near Mountainville, New York, in June 1876, naming it after his wife, the former Lucy Heywood Houghton. Homer was his guest there the following September, and visited again for an extended time in the summer and fall of 1878, when he created most of the Houghton Farm watercolors. Like the other sites he visited on his working vacations, Houghton Farm inspired a series of variations on a limited range of themes. Homer hired a boy and a girl from a local family, the Babcocks, to pose as sheepherders, and produced a large group of idyllic pastoral scenes in watercolor, from which twenty-three were submitted to the exhibition of the American Water Color Society in New York the following February. With these works Homer first gained widespread acceptance for his watercolors, the critics praising their "truth" and American subject matter. Homer's first biographer, George Sheldon, saw the Houghton Farm works as the turning point in his career.[1]

Most of the Houghton Farm works show the children tending sheep on the green, rolling hills of the farm. However, a rail fence and the stile by which one crossed it was a motif that appealed to Homer at the time, and he produced at least four views of the subject: *On the Fence* and *On the Stile*, *Feeding Time* (fig. 1), and *Spring* (fig. 2). Only two are dated, but all were likely created at about the same time, in 1878.

In spite of the critics' claims of truth, a degree of artifice was involved in the creation of the Houghton Farm watercolors. Though the boy and girl on the fence may appear to be courting, they in fact were brother and sister. Further, while the shepherdess in the Clark and

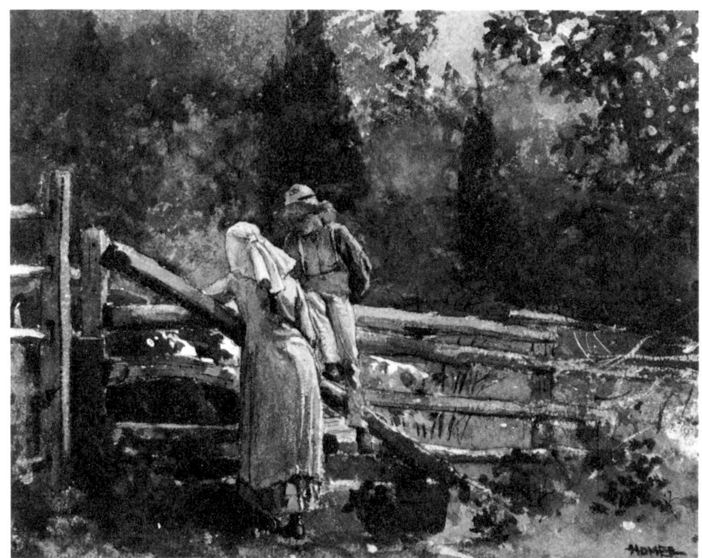

Figure 1. *Feeding Time*. Watercolor and gouache over graphite, 22.2 x 28.6 cm. Sterling and Francine Clark Art Institute, Williamstown, Massachusetts.

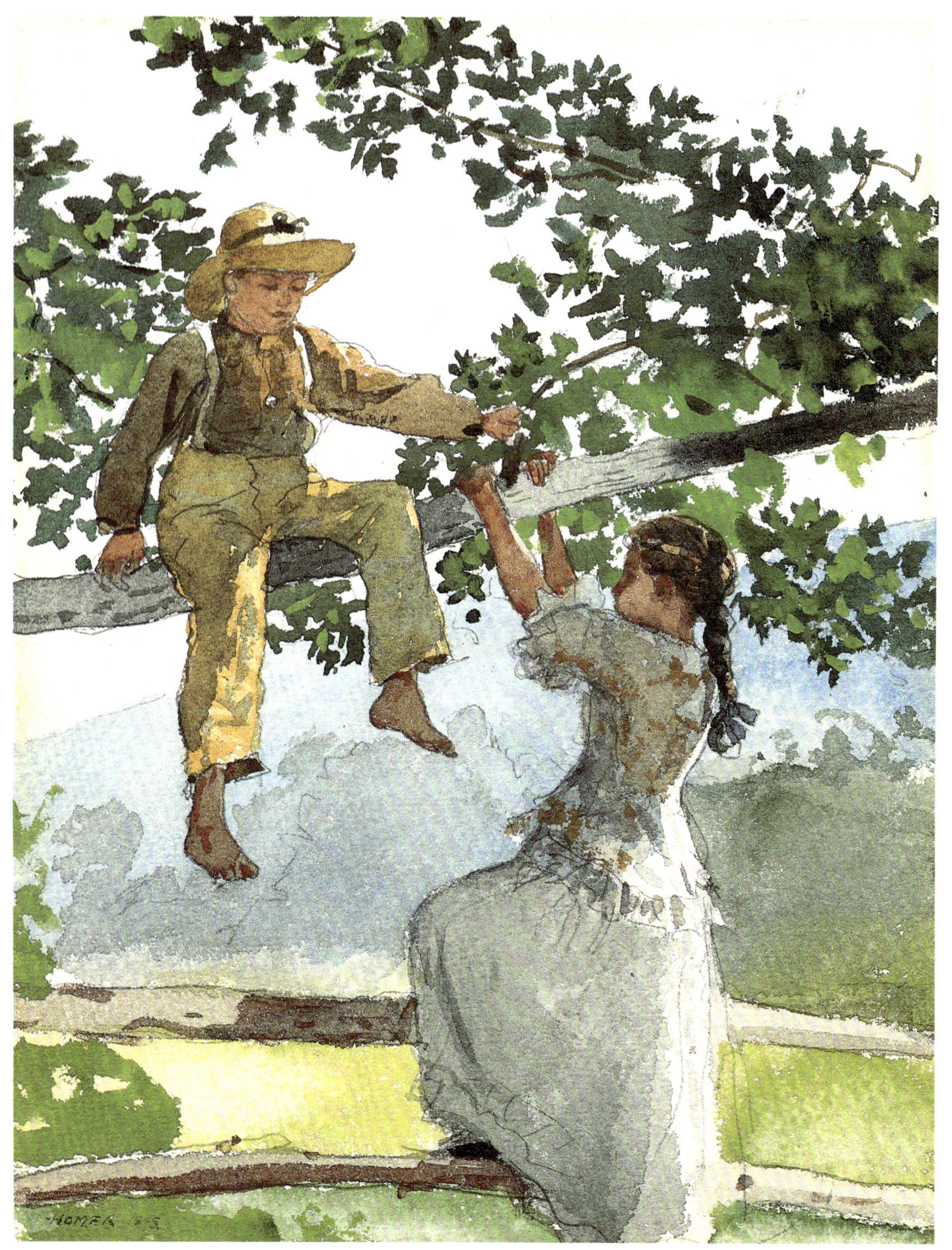

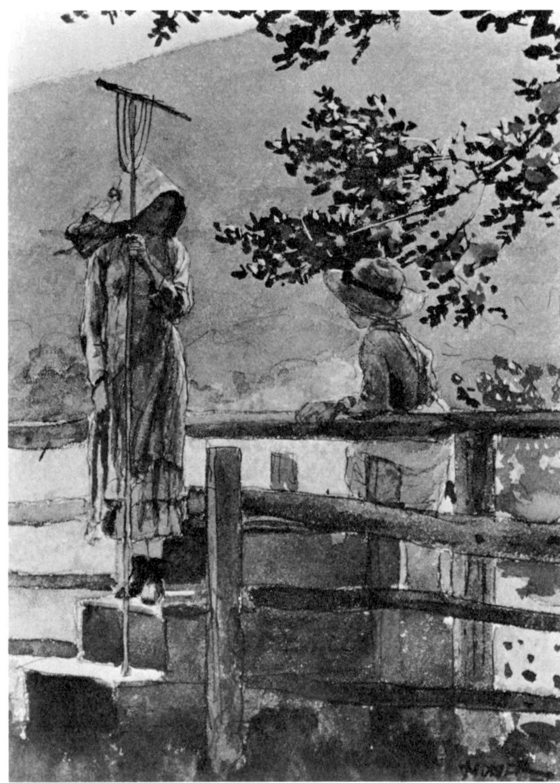

Figure 2. *Spring*, 1878. Watercolor and graphite, 28.3 x 22 cm. Collection of Rita and Daniel Fraad.

Fraad watercolors wears the loose smock and sun bonnet that were the contemporary rural attire for girls, in *On the Fence* and *On the Stile* she wears an archaic outfit of flowing white fabric, with a tight bodice and—in *On the Stile*—a beribboned straw hat, which was meant to approximate the costume of an eighteenth-century Bo-Peep. It appears that Homer brought the clothes to Mountainville and asked his model to wear them, a degree of pretense quite unusual for him. This may have been inspired by the interest in life in the eighteenth century that surrounded the celebration of the centennial two years earlier, or by the recent decorative movement, which had led Homer and a number of other artists to found the Tile Club in 1877, for nights of socializing

and tile painting. Homer depicted the Bo-Peep shepherdess on a group of tiles he decorated as a fireplace surround. It was natural for the artist to turn to such a romantic pastoral ideal for a purely ornamental project; the founding of the Tile Club and the decorative movement itself were expressions of nostalgia for ancient methods of hand craftsmanship, directed against modern mass production and anonymous machine-made ornament.

The four Houghton Farm fence pictures differ in style, indicating some technical experimentation by Homer during his time on the farm. He had been working in watercolor for five years and had gradually moved from the opaque style of his early works, with heavy use of gouache to render details and highlights, to the more delicate and luminous, though still hardly spontaneous handling of the medium that we see in the group of highly refined watercolors of women he painted in his studio in New York from 1876 to 1877. However, Homer believed strongly in the necessity of painting outside to achieve a realistic rendering of light,[2] and it seems likely that in the works created at Houghton Farm he was trying to develop a more transparent style that would exploit the intrinsic luminosity of the white paper. In *On the Fence* and *On the Stile*, broad areas are laid in with a single transparent wash, and large areas of white paper are left uncovered. Very little opaque pigment has been used and the highlights are created for the most part by allowing the natural luminosity of the paper to show through, though touches of white gouache are used to suggest light falling on the lower rails of the fence. The tonal scale and range have been drastically reduced, so that the works are very pale in overall tonality. Light and space are suggested with a remarkable economy of means, through contrasts of warm and cool colors rather than chiaroscuro, so that broad, flat, unmodulated areas of color convincingly suggest either nearby sun-washed fields or distant forested hills shrouded in hazy at-

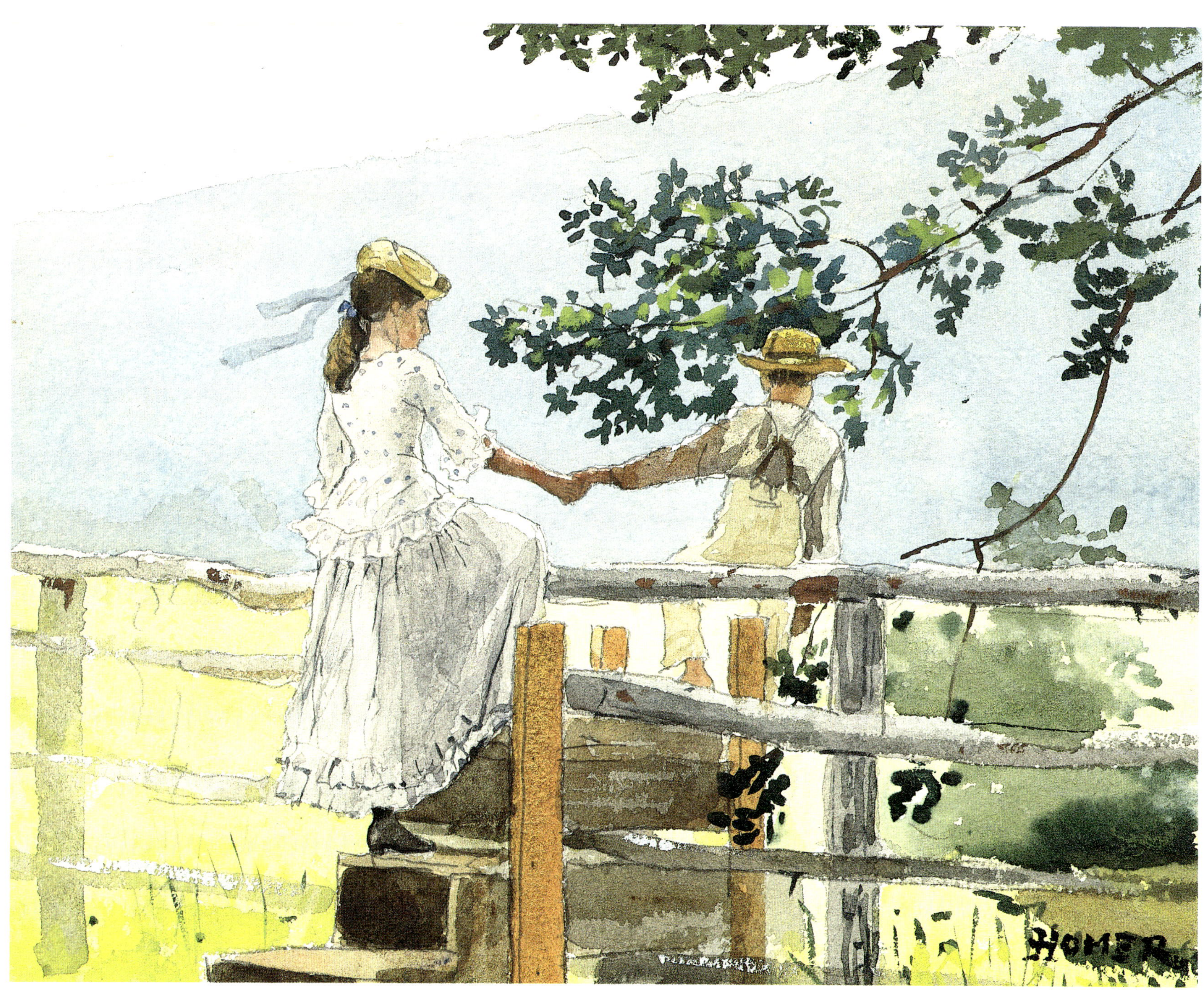
HOMER

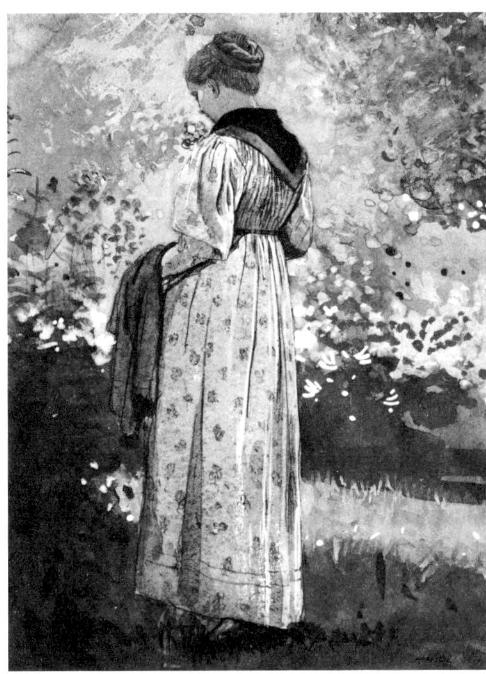

Figure 3. *In the Garden*, 1874. Watercolor, 23 x 17 cm. Collection of Diana and Arthur G. Altschul.

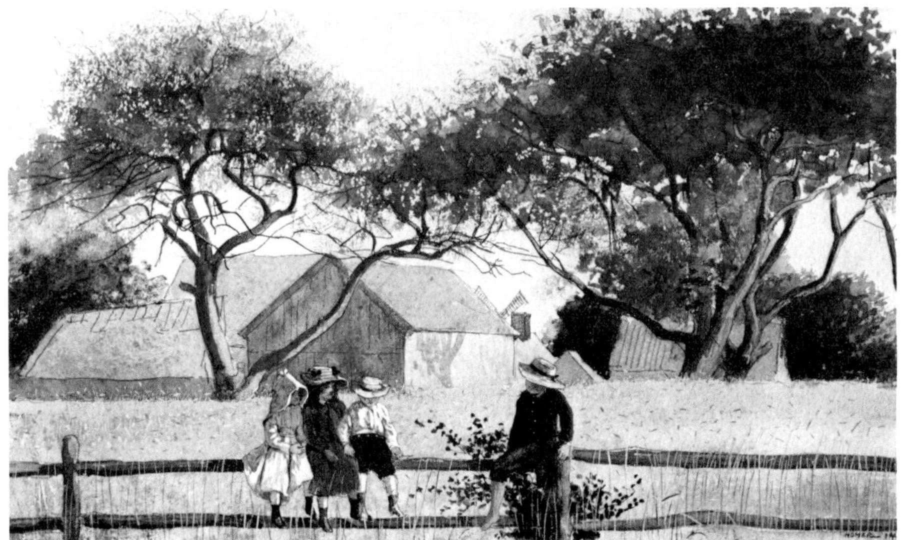

Figure 4. *Children on a Fence*, 1874. Watercolor, 17.1 x 29.2 cm. Williams College Museum of Art, Williamstown, Massachusetts.

mosphere. These flat areas of color, as well as the long sloping diagonal of the distant hill, suggest the influence of Japanese prints, which Homer would have known through his friend John LaFarge, who collected such prints and was considerably influenced by them himself.[3]

The powerful feeling of light is reinforced by the underdrawing, which is easily visible through the transparent washes. In the works of five years earlier, as exemplified by *In the Garden* (fig. 3), the drawing is firm and meticulous and adds sculptural strength and solidity to the figures. The underdrawing in *On the Fence* and *On the Stile*, by contrast, is remarkably spontaneous and notational, composed of dashes and squiggles. The lines themselves seem to reflect the shimmering, dematerializing effects of strong light. Significantly, the drawing functions only as a brief record of the observed scene, and unlike the works of five years before does not guide the later application of pigment. Form in these works is still solid and palpable—not wholly dematerialized in an ethereal haze of light as in French Impressionism—but is created through color and light alone.

Homer was particularly fond of pairs, and the meaning of his works often emerges from the opposition of elements in a composition.[4] The fence, a recurring motif in his art, can function thematically either to balance or to oppose figures or groups. The fulcrum, too, is a recurring device that functions visually and figuratively as a point of balance in Homer's work of the seventies, a period that found the artist himself poised between youth and middle age and searching for new depth and seriousness in his art.[5] A feeling of poise and balance is strong in Homer's fence pictures. In *Feeding Time* and an earlier watercolor, *Children on a Fence* (fig. 4), the figures are balanced on the fence. In the latter image this equilibrium, as well as the unequal balance of the two figural groups, is underscored by the pivoting windmill in the background. In *On the Fence*, the boy is poised precariously on a high limb above the fence, while in both *Spring* and *On the Stile*, the boy and girl are in dynamic balance on opposite sides of the fence, the rising triangle of the stile in each case functioning as a visual fulcrum. In *Feeding Time* this formal device is paralleled by the rising diagonal of the gate literally and visually giving support to the figures.

That such balance sometimes has a sexual dimension in Homer's art is made clear by the 1874 *Harper's Weekly* wood engraving *Seesaw—Gloucester, Massachusetts*, in which the girls in the foreground, seated next to a fish-net, play cat's cradle, a game of entrapment, while in the background the boys play on a seesaw, the fate of the boy at center literally in the balance as he stands uneasily poised over the fulcrum of the seesaw. Homer seems to have been preoccupied with the uneasy sexual dynamics between men and women, and especially boys and girls, at this time, since the very next engraving he published in *Harper's Weekly* was *Flirting on the Seashore and on the Meadow*, which draws a parallel between a man and woman courting on the shore and two boys flirting with a girl in a meadow. Again, a windmill in the image of adults, and a fence in the image of children, appear as symbols of this balance between the sexes. However, while *Flirting* presents a largely benign image of gender relations, *Seesaw* is redolent with a distinctly predatory quality and feeling of antagonism.

Although the models in the Houghton Farm fence pictures were brother and sister, there seems to be an underlying theme of sexual dynamics in these works. Scholars have speculated on Homer's lost love, and it has been pointed out that the red-haired woman who appears in *Shall I Tell Your Fortune?* (private collection) and the group of monumental watercolors of 1876 to 1877 disappears from the artist's work in 1878. Homer's sadness or frustration may have been subli-mated in the many scenes he painted of the solitary shepherdess, often in clinging attire, or the tender scenes of the boy and girl together on the hillsides or crossing the fence.[6]

That the Houghton Farm fence pictures might also deal with the theme of courting is suggested by their relation to one of Homer's earliest efforts in graphic art, the lithograph *Near the Broken Stile* (fig. 5), created for a music cover in 1857. Though not particularly original, having been based on the cover of the English version of the song, the lithograph bears a distinct similarity to the later *On the Stile* in the overarching trees, the fence and stile, the clasped hands of the man and woman, and even the woman's attire. It is unmistakably an image of courting, and it may have lain dormant in the artist's memory for the intervening decades before Homer created *On the Stile*.

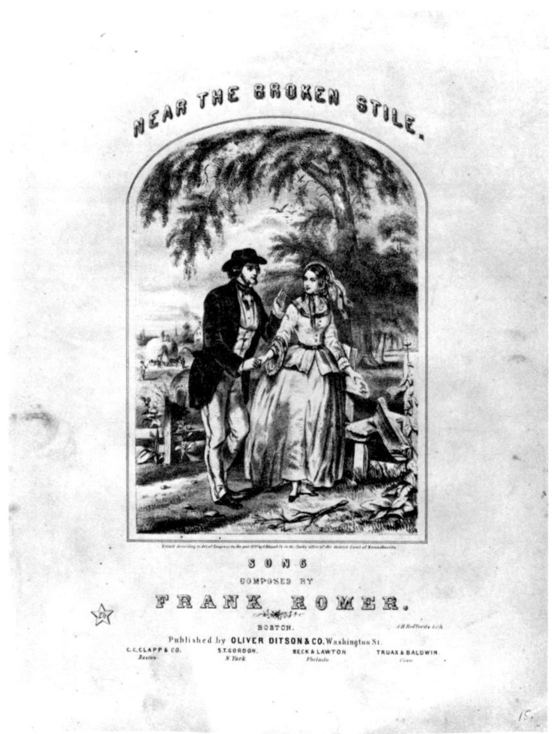

Figure 5. *Near the Broken Stile*, 1857. Lithograph, 34.3 x 26.7 cm. Sterling and Francine Clark Art Institute, Williamstown, Massachusetts.

While *On the Fence* appears to be little more than an innocent image of children at play, *Spring* crackles with sexual tension. Here the girl is distinctly higher, in a dominant position, and in a dramatic reversal of roles she has the tool—a hay rake that points threateningly at the boy in a veiled sign of aggression.[7] *Feeding Time* and *On the Stile* lie between these two in intensity. Though subtler than *Spring*, they also involve the age-old theme of the balance of the sexes. In each the boy seems to be in a position of supplication,[8] in *Feeding Time* perhaps posing a question, and in *On the Stile* in an inferior position, literally leading the girl by the hand over the fulcrum of the stile. In these scenes of childhood created at Houghton Farm, Homer explored an enduring theme in his art through new formal means.

R.W.

1. George W. Sheldon, *Hours with Art and Artists* (New York, 1882), 140; see Helen A. Cooper, *Winslow Homer Watercolors*, exhib. cat., National Gallery of Art, Amon Carter Museum, Yale University Art Gallery (Washington, D.C., 1986), 62.
2. George W. Sheldon, "Sketches and Studies II: From the Portfolios of A. H. Thayer, William M. Chase, Winslow Homer, and Peter Moran," *Art Journal*, n.s., 6 (April 1880): 105–11; quoted by Lloyd Goodrich, *Winslow Homer* (New York, 1944), 65–67.
3. The influence of Japanese prints on Homer's art has been controversial, but is now generally accepted. For a discussion, see Goodrich, *Homer*, 38; Albert Ten Eyck Gardner, *Winslow Homer, American Artist: His World and His Work* (New York, 1961), 93–118; Barbara Novak, *American Painting of the Nineteenth Century* (New York, 1969), 166–67; John Wilmerding, *Winslow Homer* (New York, 1972), 50–51; and Sally Mills, ed., *Japanese Influences in American Art*, exhib. cat., Sterling and Francine Clark Art Institute (Williamstown, Mass., 1981), 18–20.
4. For a discussion of pairs in Homer's art, see John Wilmerding, "Winslow Homer's *Right and Left*," *Studies in the History of Art* (National Gallery of Art) 9 (1980): 62–64.
5. John Wilmerding, "Winslow Homer's *Dad's Coming*," in *Essays in Honor of Paul Mellon, Collector and Benefactor*, ed. John Wilmerding (Washington, D.C., 1986), 389, 395, 400.
6. Cooper, *Homer Watercolors*, 61–62, notes the eroticism in Homer's Houghton Farm shepherdesses and suggests that they may represent a "kind of escape into rustic lyricism and the innocence of uncomplicated youth" after the failure of his affair. This manner of sublimating events in his private life into his art appears to be typical of Homer's creation. See Wilmerding, *Winslow Homer*, 26; Henry Adams, "Mortal Themes: Winslow Homer," *Art in America* 71 (February 1983): 112–26.
7. In his works of the earlier 1870s, Homer typically associated farm implements with men, as in both *Rustic Courtship* (1874, collection of Mr. and Mrs. Paul Mellon) and *Gloucester Farm* (1874, Philadelphia Museum of Art).
8. Helen Cooper observed that in Homer's images of men and women together, the men are often shown in positions of supplication. Cooper, *Homer Watercolors*, 44, 51, n. 50.

10. *Warm Afternoon (Shepherdess)*, 1878

Watercolor and graphite, 17.8 x 21.4 cm. (7 x 8⁷⁄₁₆ in.)
Signed and dated lower left: *HOMER 1878*
Private collection

11. *The Green Hill (On the Hill)*, 1878

Watercolor and graphite, 17.5 x 21 cm. (6⁷⁄₈ x 8¼ in.)
Signed and dated lower left: *HOMER 1878*
Private collection

"Winslow Homer, indeed, never fully found himself until he found the American shepherdess," wrote G. W. Sheldon in 1882.[1] The wealth of arcadian images produced by Homer during the late summer and autumn of 1878 at Lawson Valentine's Houghton Farm seemed to Sheldon and other critics a serendipitous choice of subject matter, in which the stillness of the scene allowed the artist a reflective and measured view of nature. Nearly a century later Lloyd Goodrich asserted that this group possessed "a delicacy and grace unique in all his work."[2] *Warm Afternoon* and *The Green Hill* are typical, if relatively minor, examples of the Houghton Farm harvest.[3] These bear investigation, if only because the measure of Homer's achievement lies also in the quality of his more commonplace pictures.

Since Homer hid the facial expressions of the girls in both these watercolors, a characteristic tactic of his work in this decade, their identities are difficult to establish. One or both of them may have been from the nearby Babcock family, since the artist had a Babcock girl pose as his "shepherdess." Homer apparently selected the outfits she wore as well.[4] Such artifice suggests the importance he placed on this subject matter; ultimately, their identities matter far less than the symbolic meanings they display.

These two watercolors deserve to be considered together. They are nearly identical in size, somewhat smaller than Homer's average watercolors of this period.[5] Although the artist placed no flocks upon *The Green Hill*, this work shares with *Warm Afternoon* mild slopes and shaded groves, characteristic settings of a pastoral landscape. Lost in reverie, both girls seem oblivious to their surroundings. A tranquil mood pervades.

Homer also employed a similar technique in both works. Helen Cooper has divided the Houghton Farm watercolors into two distinct groupings: those composed primarily of gouache with some transparent washes over graphite, and those painted exclusively with transparent watercolors.[6] The opaque colors used in *Warm Afternoon* and *The Green Hill*, and the effects they accomplish, place this pair in the former category. According to Cooper, "The first group is backward-looking and derives from Homer's experience as an illustrator: the lights and darks are achieved through an economy of means and the design values are clearly articulated."[7] Works like *Warm Afternoon* and *The Green Hill* rely on opaque whites for their highlights. During the 1870s Homer became drawn increasingly to the second type, "essentially pure watercolor on white paper;" these works emphasized the

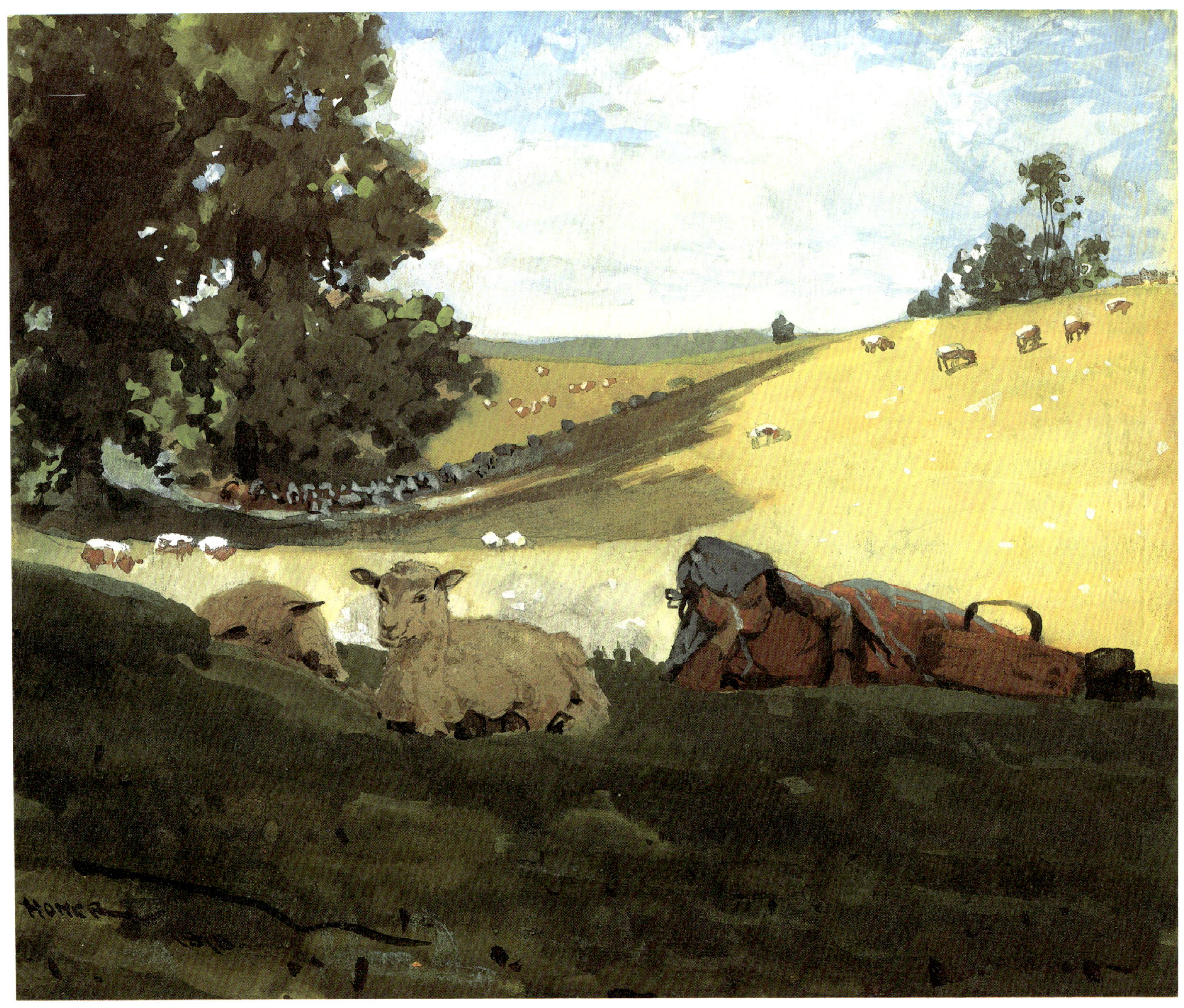
HOMER

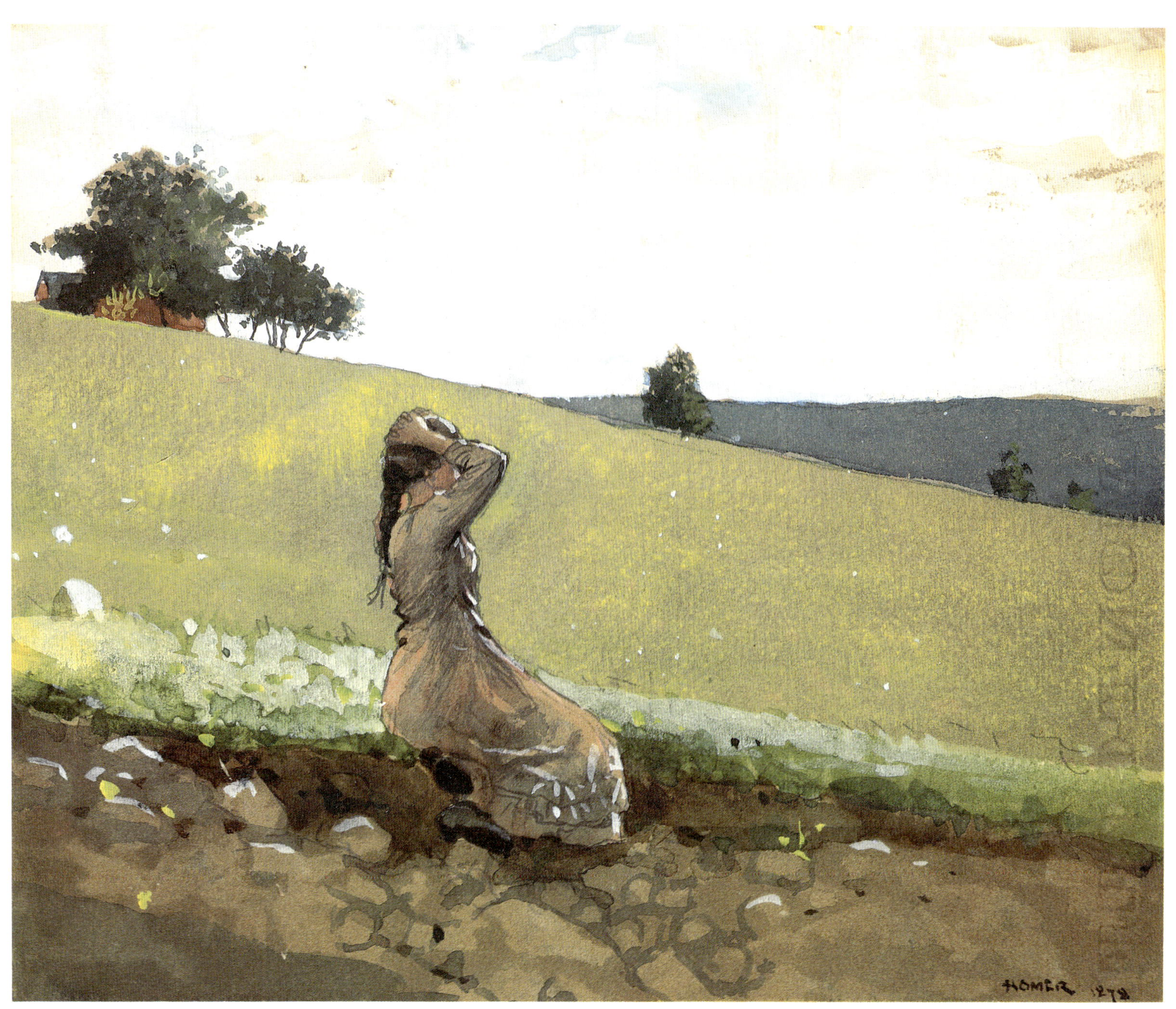
HOMER 1878

"natural luminosity of the white paper" and permitted a notable fluidity of forms, yet they required greater sureness in handling. [8]

Although *Warm Afternoon* and *The Green Hill* are more conservative in method and cautious in touch than the works in the second group, Homer displayed in this pair that he could use the gouache technique to great advantage. For instance, in *Warm Afternoon*, he depicted brilliant sunlight on the coats of the distant flocks with tiny dabs of white gouache, an effect impossible to achieve without opaque pigments. While graphite underdrawing suggests the work's initial form, Homer also used the sure line of pencil to include details like the braided hair in *The Green Hill* and the faces of the sheep in *Warm Afternoon*. Furthermore, the pastiness of gouache allowed for some measure of correction. In *Warm Afternoon*, for example, the artist eliminated some sheep in the center of the composition, evidently desiring a simpler foreground.

The thoroughness of Homer's brief absorption with shepherdess images is revealing. He experimented with two main types of figures: those in contemporary dress, as in *Warm Afternoon*, and those in deliberately archaic Bo-Peep costumes, as in *Fresh Air* (fig. 1).[9] In this work the shepherdess shares a physical resemblance with the girl of *The Green Hill*, and may in fact represent the same sitter. Homer drew and painted both of these types from different angles, depicting them in various moods and states of repose; but his interest in the shepherdess theme found significant expression in another medium, that of ceramic tiles. A founding member of New York's Tile Club, Homer began painting on eight-by-eight-inch blanks in 1877, at the club's sociable weekly meetings. Cooper has suggested that the "frenzy for decoration that swept the country following the Centennial Exhibition" prompted the choice of both medium and subject matter.[10] Significantly, Homer's most ambitious painted ceramic project was a twelve-tile fireplace surround of shepherd and shepherdess, *Pastoral* (fig. 2) of 1878, which he painted for his brother Charles, who was in business with Lawson Valentine. Using the sketches and watercolors he had made of shepherds and shepherdesses in archaic costumes, such as *Fresh Air*, Homer depicted this pair in monumental scale, totems indicating the value he placed on this subject.

Homer's Houghton Farm images of shepherdesses illustrate, more strongly than any other subject matter he chose to represent, the nostalgia then present in his work. Themes of childhood and rural life, found throughout Homer's oeuvre, were especially abundant

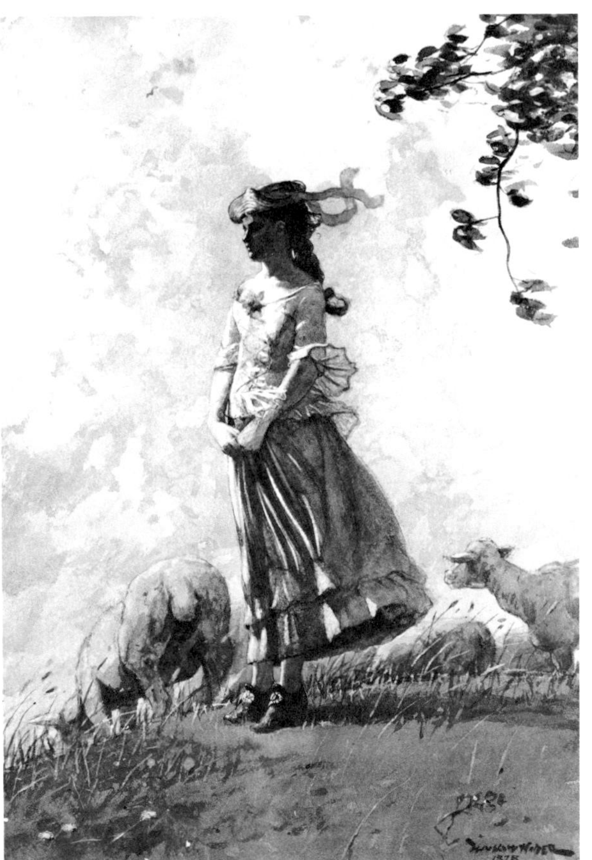

Figure 1. *Fresh Air*, 1878. Watercolor over charcoal, 51 x 35.7 cm. The Brooklyn Museum, Dick S. Ramsay Fund.

in the 1870s. In the aftermath of the Civil War, and with the coming of the 1876 Centennial Exhibition, artists like Homer turned to sentimental subjects hoping to find "a sense of permanence and continuity within the disjunction of modern life."[11] Images like *The Green Hill* and especially *Warm Afternoon*, however, by invoking the pastoral landscape tradition, took nostalgia one step further. These pictures were Homer's most explicit reference to a vanished, simpler, preindustrial past. The idealism or escapism evoked in the visual arts by such tranquil scenes with sheep found a particularly receptive audience in the nineteenth century.[12] Indeed, the presence of flocks and shepherdess gave images like *Warm Afternoon* something of an emblematic quality. Critics saw these watercolors as symbols of simplicity: "We have rarely seen anything more pure and gentle than the little American girl in the first of these sketches, half hidden away under the dark shade of the trees, with her sheep at her side."[13]

Such a reading was consistent with much nineteenth-century thought on symbolism and language. Prominent writers at mid-century reinforced the traditional attributes of abstract ideas. For example, in his enormously influential treatise *Nature*, Ralph Waldo Emerson set forth his iconography of visual and verbal signs:

It is not words only that are emblematic; it is things which are emblematic. Every natural fact is a symbol of some spiritual fact. Every appearance in nature corresponds to some state of mind, and that state of mind can only be described by presenting that natural appearance as its picture. . . . A lamb is innocence.[14]

Such thinking helps explain the appeal of Homer's shepherdess pictures, and the immediate reaction they drew. Contemporary reviewers recognized Homer's allusions to arcadian themes and responded to his motivations as well: "he strikes a singular idyllic note, something that might be termed the New England idyllic, in

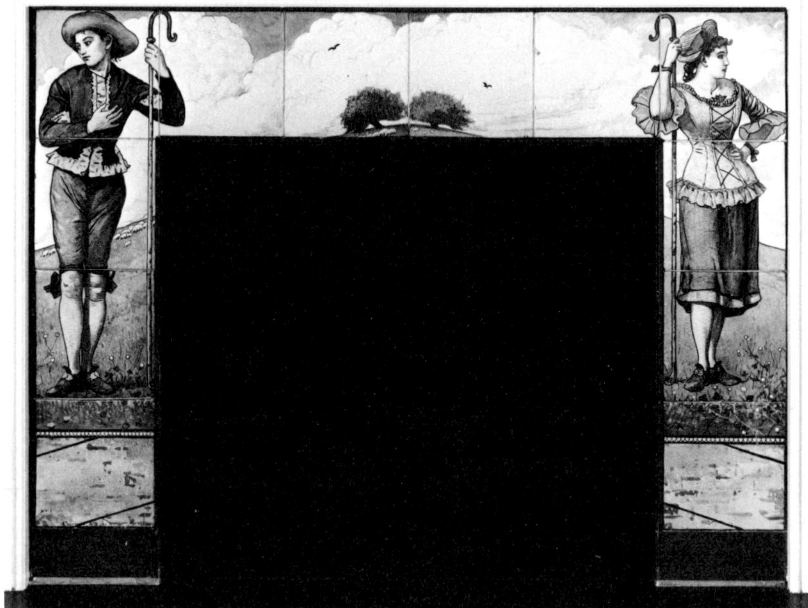

Figure 2. *Pastoral*, 1878. Ceramic tiles, 20.3 x 20.3 cm. each. Collection of Diana and Arthur G. Altschul.

order to express what is fresh and wholesome, yet a little harsh."[15] Homer addressed the pastoral tradition by treating the "little American girl" as his mythic shepherdess; this choice of subject matter successfully reconciled the artist's realist tendencies with his purely fictional theme. Moreover, the choice of subject matter in works like *Warm Afternoon* permitted the symbolic moral virtue of rural life to be combined with the artistic truth Homer found in outdoor painting.

F.I.

1. George W. Sheldon, *Hours with Art and Artists* (New York, 1882), 140.

2. Lloyd Goodrich, "Winslow Homer in New York State," *Art in America* 52 (April 1964): 80.

3. For examples of shepherdesses in watercolor, see Helen A. Cooper, *Winslow Homer Watercolors*, exhib. cat., National Gallery of Art, Amon Carter Museum, Yale University Art Gallery (Washington, D.C., 1986),

figs. 40–43, 48. She discusses the Houghton Farm watercolors at length on pp. 52–65. The Cooper-Hewitt Museum, New York, has a sizeable number of pencil-and-wash studies of sheep and shepherdesses from 1878. John Wilmerding and Elaine Evans Dee, *Winslow Homer 1836–1910: A Selection from the Cooper-Hewitt Collection, Smithsonian Institution*, exhib. cat. (Washington, D.C., 1972), no. 34, provides a typical sheet.

4. Gordon Hendricks, *The Life and Work of Winslow Homer* (New York, 1979), 138.

5. Helen Cooper estimated the majority of the Houghton Farm watercolors to be approximately 9 x 12 in.; Cooper, *Homer Watercolors*, 55.

6. Ibid., 55.

7. Ibid., 55–56.

8. Ibid., 57.

9. Ibid., 56–62. *Fresh Air* was once owned by Lawson Valentine's brother, Henry C. Valentine; see Appendix.

10. Cooper, *Homer Watercolors*, 60.

11. Ibid., 54. Cooper refers to Robert L. Herbert, "City vs. Country: The Rural Image in French Painting from Millet to Gauguin," *Artforum 8* (February 1970): 44–55, which, although concerned with France, nonetheless presents informative parallels with American interest in rural painting in Homer's day.

12. John Barrel, *The Dark Side of the Landscape: The Rural Poor in English Painting 1730–1840* (Cambridge, 1980). Although this study deals with England, and focuses on an earlier period, it discusses at some length the motivations that guided the painting of rural images, particularly in regard to issues of social class. Robert C. Cafritz, Lawrence Gowing, David Rosand, *Places of Delight: The Pastoral Landscape*, exhib. cat., The Phillips Collection (Washington, D.C., 1988), 182–248, provides a formalist overview of pastoral subjects in nineteenth- and twentieth-century art.

13. S. N. Carter, "The Water-Colour Exhibition," *The Art Journal* 5 (March 1879): 94.

14. Ralph Waldo Emerson, "Nature" (1849) in *Essays and Lectures* (New York, 1983), 20.

15. "The Watercolor Society: A Brilliant Show at the Twelfth Exhibition," *New York Times*, February 1, 1879, 5.

APPENDIX

(Asterisks indicate works included in the exhibition.)

WORKS BY WINSLOW HOMER

OWNED BY LAWSON VALENTINE

Study for "The Bright Side," 1864. Oil on paper, 16.5 x 20.9 cm. (6½ x 8¼ in.). Collection of J. Nicholson.

**Sketch for "The Bright Side" and "Army Teamsters,"* 1864. Graphite, wash, and white heightening, 17.8 x 25.4 cm. (7 x 10 in.). Private collection.

**Army Teamsters,* 1866. Oil on canvas, 44.8 x 71.7 cm. (17⅝ x 28¼ in.). Private collection. An 1889 chromolithograph of this painting was used as an advertisement for Valentine's company.

The Trapper (Adirondack Lake), 1870. Oil on canvas, 49.5 x 74.9 cm. (19½ x 29½ in.). Colby College Museum.

**Berry Pickers,* July 1873. Watercolor, graphite, and gouache, 24.8 x 35.2 cm. (9¾ x 13⅞ in.). Private collection.

**Boys Wading,* 1873. Watercolor and gouache over graphite, 24.8 x 34.9 cm. (9¾ x 13¾ in.). Private collection.

**The Flirt,* 1874. Oil on panel, 20.6 x 31.4 cm. (8⅛ x 12⅜ in.). Private collection.

**A Sick Chicken,* 1874. Watercolor, graphite, and gouache, 24.8 x 19.7 cm. (9¾ x 7¾ in.). Private collection.

A Farm Team (A Hilltop Barn), May 14, 1874. Watercolor, 20.9 x 33 cm. (8¼ x 13 in.) (sight). Location unknown.

Four Bicyclists Racing, ca. 1874. Drawing, 18 x 25 cm. (7⅛ x 9⅞ in.). Private collection. The word VALENTINE appears on a sign.

Boy on Bicycle, Boy on Mule, Valentine Factory in Background, ca. 1874. Drawing, 18.7 x 25 cm. (7⅜ x 9⅞ in.). Private collection. The word *Valentine* appears on the factory and on one of the envelopes flying through the air.

Girl with a Straw in Her Mouth, 1875. Black chalk on blue paper with opaque white, 17.1 x 22.9 cm. (6¾ x 9 in.). Colby College Muse-um. Gordon Hendricks believed that this depicts Mary Chamberlain Valentine.

Domestic Chores, ca. 1875. Graphite, two drawings on one sheet, 26.7 x 19 cm. (10½ x 7½ in.). Special Collections, Colby College, Waterville, Maine.Waterville, Maine.

Houghton Farm: Lady with Poodle, September 24, 1876. Pen and ink, 20.9 x 13.6 cm. (8¼ x 5⅜ in.). Special Collections, Colby College, Waterville, Maine.

**Almira Houghton Valentine and Mary Chamberlain Valentine,* 1877. Oil on canvas, 57.8 x 45 cm. (22¾ x 17¾ in.). Wadsworth Atheneum. Gift of the Lawson Valentine Foundation.

Game, before 1878. Oil, size and location unknown.

Tending Sheep, Houghton Farm, ca. 1878. Watercolor, 20.9 x 27.6 cm. (8¼ x 10⅞ in.). Location unknown.

Weary, ca. 1878. Watercolor, 21.9 x 28.6 cm. (8⅝ x 11¼ in.). Daniel J. Terra Collection, Terra Museum of American Art.

**On the Fence (On the Farm),* 1878. Watercolor and gouache over graphite, 28.6 x 22.1 cm. (11¼ x 8¹¹⁄₁₆ in.). Private collection.

**On the Stile,* ca. 1878. Watercolor over graphite, 22 x 28.2 cm. (8¹¹⁄₁₆ x 11⅛ in.). Private collection.

Pond and Willows, Houghton Farm, 1878. Watercolor, 17.8 x 20.9 cm. (7 x 8¼ in.). Location unknown.

Plowing (Horse and Plowman, Houghton Farm), ca. 1878. Watercolor, 15.9 x 27.9 cm. (6¼ x 11 in.). Location unknown.

Sheep and Cattle, Houghton Farm, 1878. Watercolor, 17.5 x 20.6 cm. (6⅞ x 8⅛ in.). Location unknown.

A Shady Spot, Houghton Farm, 1878. Watercolor, 17.5 x 20.6 cm. (6⅞ x 8⅛ in.). Location unknown.

The Shepherd Girl, Houghton Farm, 1878. Watercolor, 17.1 x 20.9 cm. (6¾ x 8¼ in.). Location unknown.

**Warm Afternoon* (*Shepherdess*), 1878. Watercolor and graphite, 17.8 x 21.4 cm. (7 x 8⁷⁄₁₆ in.). Private collection.

The Shy Sweethearts, 1878. Watercolor, 29.9 x 22.2 cm. (11¾ x 8¾ in.). Location unknown.

The Flock of Sheep, Houghton Farm, 1878. Watercolor, 20.6 x 27.3 cm. (8⅛ x 10¾ in.). Private collection.

Four Leaf Clover, Houghton Farm, ca. 1878. Watercolor, 17 x 29.7 cm. (6¹¹⁄₁₆ x 11¹¹⁄₁₆ in.). Location unknown.

**The Green Hill* (*On the Hill*), 1878. Watercolor and graphite, 17.5 x 21 cm. (6⅞ x 8¼ in.). Private collection.

Cow in Pasture, 1878. Watercolor, 17.2 x 29.2 cm. (6¾ x 11½ in.). Location unknown.

The Shepherdess, 1879. Oil, 57.2 x 38.1 cm. (22½ x 15 in.). Private collection, Pacific Palisades, California.

Horse, 1879. Drawing, size and location unknown.

Young Woman, 1880. Watercolor, 24.5 x 34.9 cm. (9⅝ x 13¾ in.). The Strong Museum, Rochester, New York.

Lucy Houghton Valentine, 1883. Oil on canvas, 57.5 x 44.5 cm. (22⅝ x 17½ in.). Collection of Richard Namon.

The Ship's Boat, ca. 1884. Pen, black ink, and black crayon on cardboard, 22 x 41.9 cm. (8⅝ x 16½ in.). New Britain Museum of American Art. This and other pen-and-ink drawings by Homer descended in the family of Mary Chamberlain Valentine.

Reading a Letter, n.d. Watercolor, 24.8 x 18.7 cm. (9¾ x 7⅜ in.). Location unknown.

Mending Toy Boats (?), June 1873. Graphite and white wash, 22.9 x 32.7 cm. (9 x 12⅞ in.). Private collection. This came from the Pulsifer family.

Schooners (?), 1880. Watercolor, 21 x 33.3 cm. (8¼ x 13⅛ in.). Location unknown.

Girl at Gloucester (?), 1880. Watercolor, 25.1 x 34.6 cm. (9⅞ x 13⅝ in.). Location unknown.

OWNED BY HENRY C. VALENTINE

Grace Hoops (*Grace Playing Hoops*), November 14, 1872. Oil sketch, 30.8 x 18.1 cm. (12⅛ x 7⅛ in.). Location unknown.

Milkmaid, 1878. Watercolor, 49.5 x 34.3 cm. (19½ x 13½ in.). National Gallery of Art.

The Reaper (*Reaping the Field*), 1878. Watercolor, 50.8 x 35.6 cm. (20 x 14 in.). Location unknown.

Shepherdess Tending Sheep, 1878. Watercolor, 28.3 x 49.5 cm. (11⅛ x 19½ in.). The Brooklyn Museum.

Fresh Air, 1878. Watercolor over charcoal, 51 x 35.7 cm. (20¹⁄₁₆ x 14¹⁄₁₆ in.). The Brooklyn Museum.

Girl Seated in a Grove, 1880. Watercolor, 24.5 x 34 cm. (9⅝ x 13⅜ in.). Location unknown.

Fishergirls (*Fishergirls Coiling Tackle*), 1881. Watercolor, 43.2 x 58.4 cm. (17 x 23 in.). Collection of Ogden Mills Phipps.

Undertow, ca. 1886. Etching, 16.8 x 25.4 cm. (6⅝ x 10 in.). Sterling and Francine Clark Art Institute.

Miss Susie Valentine (*Looking Out to Sea*), August 24, 1900. Graphite and black crayon, page size: 20.3 x 15.9 cm. (8 x 6¼ in.). Location unknown. Inscribed to Susie Valentine, daughter of Henry Valentine, who spent several summers at Prout's Neck.

The Oyster Fishermen, n.d. Graphite and Chinese white, 9.2 x 22.5 cm. (3⅝ x 8⅞ in.). Location unknown.

OWNED BY NATHAN TROWBRIDGE PULSIFER

House, Santiago, Cuba, ca. 1885. Watercolor, 34.9 x 50.2 cm. (13¾ x 19¾ in.). Location unknown.

A Volante on a Mountain Road (*Calash, Cuba* or *A Ride in the Surrey*), 1885. Watercolor, 33 x 50.8 cm. (13 x 20 in.). Location unknown.

Skating, mid- to late 1860s. Oil, size and location unknown. Descended in the family of Charles E. Morrill, who opened a branch of Valentine & Company in Chicago in the 1870s. It merged with the parent company in 1899; Morrill became president the following year.

Looking for the Boys (*Above the Sea, Tynemouth*), ca. 1881–82. Watercolor, 34.3 x 47.6 cm. (13½ x 18¾ in.). Location unknown. Homer gave this to William B. Long (who was connected with Valentine & Company). Long visited Homer in Cullercoats, England.

Boys Beside a Lake (*Boys on Rocks*), probably 1860s. Watercolor, 17.5 x 24.3 cm. (6⅞ x 9⁹⁄₁₆ in.). Location unknown. Probably given by Mr. and Mrs. Charles Homer to William "Hadwin" Houghton, stepbrother of Lucy Houghton Valentine and affiliated with Valentine & Company.

L.A.

SELECTED BIBLIOGRAPHY

Adams, Henry. "Mortal Themes: Winslow Homer." *Art in America* 71 (February 1983): 112–26.

———. "Winslow Homer's Mystery Woman." *Art & Antiques* (November 1984): 38–45.

Beam, Philip C. *Winslow Homer's Magazine Engravings*. New York and London, 1979.

Cikovsky, Nicolai, Jr. "Winslow Homer's *Prisoners from the Front*." *Metropolitan Museum Journal* 12 (1977): 155–72.

———. "Winslow Homer's *School Time*: 'A Picture Thoroughly National'." In *Essays in Honor of Paul Mellon, Collector and Benefactor*. Edited by John Wilmerding. Washington, D.C., 1986, 46–69.

Cooper, Helen A. *Winslow Homer Watercolors*. Exhib. cat., National Gallery of Art, Amon Carter Museum, Yale University Art Gallery. Washington, D.C., 1986.

Curry, David Park. *Winslow Homer: The Croquet Game*. Exhib. cat., Yale University Art Gallery. New Haven, 1984.

Downes, William H. *The Life and Works of Winslow Homer*. Boston and New York, 1911.

Gardner, Albert Ten Eyck. *Winslow Homer, American Artist: His World and His Work*. New York, 1961.

Gelman, Barbara, ed. *The Wood Engravings of Winslow Homer*. New York, 1969.

Goodrich, Lloyd. *Winslow Homer*. New York, 1944.

———. *Winslow Homer in New York State*. Exhib. cat., Storm King Art Center. Mountainville, N. Y., 1963. Reprint, *Art in America* 52 (April 1964): 78–87.

Green, Samuel M. *The Harold Trowbridge Pulsifer Collection of Winslow Homer Paintings and Drawings at Colby College*. Waterville, Maine, 1949.

Grossman, Julian. *Echo of a Distant Drum: Winslow Homer and the Civil War*. New York, n.d.

Hendricks, Gordon. *The Life and Work of Winslow Homer*. New York, 1979.

Hoopes, Donelson F. *Winslow Homer Watercolors*. New York, 1969.

Murphy, Alexandra R., Rafael Fernandez, and Jennifer Gordon. *Winslow Homer in the Clark Collection*. Exhib. cat., Sterling and Francine Clark Art Institute. Williamstown, Mass., 1986.

Novak, Barbara. *American Painting of the Nineteenth Century*. New York, 1969.

Sheldon, George W. "American Painters—Winslow Homer and F. A. Bridgeman." *Art Journal*, n.s., 4 (August 1878): 225–29. Reprint, with revisions, in *American Painters*. New York, 1879 (enlarged edition, 1881, 25–29).

———. "Sketches and Studies II: From the Portfolios of A. H. Thayer, William M. Chase, Winslow Homer, and Peter Moran." *Art Journal*, n.s., 6 (April 1880): 105–11. Reprint, with revisions, in *Hours with Art and Artists*. New York, 1882: 132–41.

Simpson, Marc, et al. *Winslow Homer: Paintings of the Civil War*. Exhib. cat., The Fine Arts Museums of San Francisco, Portland Museum of Art, Amon Carter Museum (San Francisco, 1988).

Wilmerding, John. *Winslow Homer*. New York, 1972.

———. "Winslow Homer's *Right and Left*." *Studies in the History of Art* (National Gallery of Art) 9 (1980): 59–85.

———. "Winslow Homer's *Dad's Coming*." In *Essays in Honor of Paul Mellon, Collector and Benefactor*. Edited by John Wilmerding. Washington, D.C., 1986, 388–401.

Wilson, Christopher Kent. "Winslow Homer's *The Veteran in a New Field*: A Study of the Harvest Metaphor and Popular Culture." *American Art Journal* 17 (Autumn, 1985): 2–27.

Wood, Peter H. and Karen C. C. Dalton. *Winslow Homer's Images of Blacks: The Civil War and Reconstruction Years*. Exhib. cat., the Menil Collection, Virginia Museum of Fine Arts, North Carolina Museum of Art. Austin, 1988.